THE ULTIMATE
30 MINUTES OR LESS
COOKBOOK

The paper in this printing meets the requirements of the ANSI Standard Z39.48-1992.

While every care has been taken in compiling the recipes for this book, the publisher, Cogin, Inc., or any other person who has been involved in working on this publication assumes no responsibility or liability for any errors or omissions, inadvertent or not, that may be found in the recipes or text, nor for any problems or damages that may arise as a result of preparing these recipes.

If food allergies or dietary restrictions are a concern, it is recommended that you carefully read ingredient product labels as well as consult a nutritionist or your physician to determine if a particular recipe meets your dietary needs.

We encourage you to use caution when working with all kitchen equipment and to always follow food safety guidelines.

To purchase this book for business or promotional use or to purchase more than 50 copies at a discount, or for custom editions, please contact Cogin, Inc. at the address below or info@mrfood.com.

Inquiries should be addressed to:
Cogin, Inc.
1770 NW 64 Street, Suite 500
Fort Lauderdale, FL 33309

ISBN-10: 0-9981635-0-3

Printed in the United States of America
Second Edition
www.MrFood.com

Other titles you may enjoy from the Mr. Food Test Kitchen:

Christmas Made Easy
Quick & Easy Comfort Cookbook
Sinful Sweets & Tasty Treats
Just One More Bite!
Hello Taste, Goodbye Guilt!
Cook it Slow, Cook it Fast
Guilt-Free Weeknight Favorites
Wheel of Fortune Collectible Cookbook
The Ultimate Cooking for Two Cookbook
The Ultimate Cake Mix & More Cookbook

Introduction

With so much hustle and bustle in our daily lives, we could all use some quick and easy ideas for getting food on the table. However, most of us aren't willing to sacrifice on taste or quality just to save a little time. So, what's the solution? Well, it's in your hands! After over 40 years of providing you with recipes that are both quick and easy, we decided to go the extra mile by challenging ourselves to create a cookbook full of recipes that can be prepped and cooked in 30 minutes or less. And as you've probably guessed by now, we did it!

As we all know, Americans are spending less time preparing home-cooked meals than they did thirty years ago. That's because most of us have busier schedules than folks did back then; some people just feel like they don't have the time to cook. Well, it's time to set aside that excuse! You see, in this cookbook we've packed more than 130 recipes that are perfect for everyone from the busy mom or dad, to the college student with the loaded schedule, or even the retired senior who just wants to put a good meal on the table without having to give up lots of time. Each recipe, from prep to plate, truly takes 30 minutes or less. And, as you've come to expect from the Mr. Food Test Kitchen, we've thoroughly tested every single one to make sure it not only tastes good, but it's easy enough for anyone to make.

Before creating this cookbook, we came across other cookbooks that claimed to have 30-minute recipes. What we found was that many of them could be cooked within that time frame, but that most of them didn't consider prep times, chill times, or any other miscellaneous steps necessary to getting the dish done. To them, a 30-minute recipe meant only that it would be cooked in 30 minutes. Well, that's not the way we think! We actually used timers in the test kitchen to ensure that every recipe could be done in 30 minutes, from the moment we gathered our ingredients to the time it was ready to be plated. And yes, we did have to part with a few recipes that took just a minute too long (you may see them in another book!), but that's only because we wanted to truly deliver the book you've been dreaming of forever.

Imagine cooking up a comforting meatloaf, a satisfying skillet casserole, or roasted chicken all within a half hour. Typically, you'd expect these types of dishes to take hours, but we've figured out a way to reduce the time, so your family can enjoy these on any busy weeknight. One forkful of any of these recipes and you'll understand what makes this cookbook so great—we cut the cooking time, but not the flavor! And since no meal is complete without dessert, you can bet that we've included lots of sweet treats that are also done in less time than it takes to watch the evening news. No sweet tooth will be able to resist our decadent cakes, praiseworthy pies, and bubblin' hot cobblers.

Not only does every recipe feature step-by-step instructions that are easy to follow, but we've made sure to include a full-page photo for each one, to help get your taste buds tingling. There's really no reason to skip on making home-cooked meals now!

So, what do you say we get going and start making some marvelous meals for yourself and your family? It won't take long (30 minutes or less to be exact!) before you'll be saying...

"OOH IT'S SO GOOD!!®"

Acknowledgements

Who would think that it would take so many people to create a cookbook for two? We sure wouldn't have if we hadn't worked on it ourselves. But the reality is that it does, and we are so thankful that we've assembled such a talented team over the years.

Patty Rosenthal
Test Kitchen Director

Kelly Rusin
Photographer & Stylist

Howard Rosenthal
Chief Food Officer

Jodi Flayman
Director of Publishing

Merly Mesa
Editor

Carol Ginsburg
Editor

Amy Magro
Dir. of Business Affairs

Jaime Gross
Business Assistant

Yolanda Reid
Brand Ambassador

Steve Ginsburg
Chief Executive Officer

Dave DiCarlo
Test Kitchen Assistant

Ana Cook
Website Editor

Roxana DeLima
Comptroller

Hal Silverman
Post Production
Hal Silverman Studio

Lorraine Dan
Book Design
Grand Design

Table of Contents

Hints & Tips

Now that you have this book in your hands and you've flipped through the pages, we know you can't wait to start cooking. But before you do, please take a few minutes to read through some hints and tips we've assembled for you, to ensure that every recipe comes out picture-perfect, tastes amazing, and is done lickety-split.

- **Read It Through:** Before you start making any recipe, in this or any other cookbook, take a moment and read through the entire recipe before starting it. That way you'll have a better understanding of the whole process and can best manage your time.

- **Gather Your Ingredients:** There's nothing more frustrating when cooking than to discover you're missing an ingredient halfway through the recipe. That's why we suggest you gather all the ingredients listed on the recipe before you start. This will save you time and prevent any unnecessary cooking headaches.

- **Multitasking:** You will see in our recipes that we use the term, "meanwhile" when we suggest that you do one task while you're waiting for another one to be finished. An example of this would be "Cook the pasta for 6 to 8 minutes or until tender. Meanwhile, chop the veggies for the sauce." Rather than standing there waiting for the pasta to cook, you work on the next step, which is another great timesaver.

- **Keep Your Kitchen Organized:** Don't waste time in the kitchen by searching for this and that when you need it. Make sure you keep pots and pans, utensils, and other cooking essentials organized. We love scavenger hunts, but not when we're trying to cook.

- **Produce Shortcuts:** As always, we believe that using the right shortcut products can save lots of time. So, rather than peeling garlic and chopping it, why not buy pre-chopped garlic? And although we love starting out with fresh-from-the-garden veggies, it can sometimes be quite time consuming to deal with all it takes to get them ready for a recipe. That's why we love the convenience of frozen veggies. You see, since we can buy them just the way we need them (chopped, cut into florets, diced, etc.), it save us lots of time. Plus, if we keep our freezer stocked with a variety of them, we can just use what we need, and keep the rest frozen until we need them again, which helps reduce food waste.

- **Grocery Store Timesavers:** Today, with good quality products in our supermarkets, it's ok to use packaged shortcuts from time to time. For example, why drag out the canisters of flour, sugar, and such when we can start with a boxed cake mix? And sure, we can make our own breadcrumbs, but who has time for that on a busy weeknight, when there are so many great varieties available at the supermarket? You get the idea! Oh, and don't worry—when we tested these recipes, we made sure not to sacrifice taste or quality just to save time. The timesaving ingredients we suggest in our recipes all delivered superior results.

- **Face It Forward:** It may seem silly to you now, but trust us on this one. When you put your groceries away, organize them so that the front labels of your cans and packages face you. This will reduce the amount of time spent digging through the pantry trying to decipher the cat food from the tuna fish. Every minute counts!

- **Keep Your Knives Sharp:** Did you know that you're more likely to cut yourself with a dull knife than with a sharp one? With sharp knives, the blade goes where you want it and stays there. When your knives are dull, the cutting edge will often slip and...well, you better watch out for your fingers! By keeping your knife blades sharp, you'll save time, especially since you won't have to stop making dinner to find the first-aid kit.

- **Use a Timer:** There's no reason to guess on cooking time when the recipe lists it. And since you'll be multitasking, make sure you set a timer, so you stay on track. There's no bigger time-waster than burning dinner and then having to start over... or having to wait for a pizza to be delivered.

- **Reduce Steps:** Sure, we all want to add steps to our day to make sure we stay healthy, but not when we're in the kitchen. So, rather than making endless trips to the trash can, how about keeping a large "trash" bowl on your counter? This way, you can peel your potatoes over it, toss in your onion trimmings, and so on. And don't forget to keep a kitchen towel within reach. Not only is it convenient to wipe your hands, but it's also perfect for those "Oops! I spilled a little" moments.

As always, we remember our founder, Art Ginsburg, who believed that everyone would cook if only we could make it "quick & easy." We thank you for allowing us to carry on this tradition.

Welcome to the Mr. Food Test Kitchen Family!

Whether you've been a fan of the Mr. Food Test Kitchen for years or were just recently introduced to us, we want to welcome you into our kitchen...and our family. Even though we've grown in many ways over the years, the one thing that hasn't changed is our philosophy for quick & easy cooking...and baking.

Over forty years ago we began by sharing our recipes with you through the television screen. Today, not only is the Mr. Food Test Kitchen TV segment syndicated all over the country, but we've also proudly published over 50 best-selling cookbooks. That's not to mention the hugely popular MrFood.com and EverydayDiabeticRecipes.com. And for those of you who love to get social, we do too! You can find us online on Facebook, Twitter, Pinterest, and Instagram—boy, do we love connecting with you!

If you've got a passion for baking (like we do!), then you know that the only thing better than curling up with a cookbook and drooling over the pictures is actually getting to taste the finished recipes. That's why we give you simple step-by-step instructions that make it feel like we're in your kitchen guiding you along the way. Your taste buds will be celebrating in no time!

By the way, now that you're part of the family, we want to let you in on a little secret...we recently launched all sorts of tools and bakeware to make your life in the kitchen even easier. Be sure to let your friends and family know, 'cause once everyone gets word of it, we're not sure how long they'll stay on the shelves!

So whether you're new to the family or you've been a part of it from the beginning, we want to thank you. You can bet there is always room at our table for you, because there's nothing better than sharing in all of the..."OOH IT'S SO GOOD!!®"

Lightning-Quick Breakfasts

Glazed Doughnut Bacon 'n' Egg Sandwiches

Okay, we're going to need you to choose a day where you forget about the calories and let yourself indulge. Then, on that day, start your morning with this beauty of a breakfast sandwich. Two slices of crispy-cooked bacon, a perfect fried egg, and yummy cheddar cheese sandwiched between a glazed doughnut? It's hard not to drool just talking about it!

Serves 2

Ingredients

2 glazed doughnuts

4 slices bacon

1 tablespoon butter

2 eggs

2 slices cheddar cheese

Preparation

1 Cut doughnuts in half horizontally; set aside.

2 In a large skillet over medium heat, cook bacon 6 to 8 minutes, or until crispy; drain on paper towels. Wipe skillet clean. Melt butter over medium heat and fry eggs until firm; flip, then cook 1 more minute.

3 Place 1 egg on the bottom half of each doughnut, top each with 2 slices bacon, and a slice of cheese. Place doughnut top over each and serve.

Test Kitchen Tip: *The heat from the hot egg will melt the cheese slightly, which makes it just the right amount of gooey.*

The Ultimate Breakfast Nachos

Nachos aren't just for snacking on at the movies or on game days. Nowadays, you can eat nachos morning, noon, and night, so long as you combine the right ingredients. For breakfast we like to make sure we get all the good stuff in; we're talkin' eggs, sausage, bacon, cheese, salsa...the ultimate combo. What do you think—did we miss anything?

Serves 6

Ingredients

6 cups tortilla chips

4 large eggs

1 tablespoon water

2 tablespoons butter

2 cooked breakfast sausage links, microwaved according to package directions, sliced

¼ cup ready-to-serve bacon pieces

1 cup salsa

1 cup shredded cheddar cheese

1 scallion, sliced

Preparation

1 Preheat oven to 425 degrees F. Place tortilla chips on a baking sheet that's been lined with aluminum foil; set aside.

2 In a medium bowl, whisk eggs and water.

3 In a medium skillet over medium heat, melt butter; add egg mixture and scramble until firm. Spoon mixture over tortilla chips. Top with sausage, bacon, salsa, and cheese.

4 Bake 3 to 5 minutes, or until cheese is melted. Sprinkle with scallions and serve.

So Many Options: *You can make this as meaty as you like by adding some sliced pepperoni, or some chopped up ham right along with the sausage.*

Perfect Poached Eggs & Avocado Toast

Avocado toast is really the people's choice of healthy breakfast foods. It's simple, it's quick, and it's loaded with good fats and lots of fiber. To make ours even better, we top it off with a perfect poached egg. A sprinkle of pepper and a drizzle of hot sauce add the finishing touches to this delightfully delicious breakfast.

Serves 2

Ingredients

5 cups water

1 tablespoon white vinegar

2 avocados, pitted

1 teaspoon lemon juice

¼ teaspoon salt

4 eggs

4 slices whole grain bread

Coarsely ground black pepper for sprinkling

Sriracha for drizzling

Preparation

1 In a medium skillet, bring water and vinegar to a boil.

2 Meanwhile, in a medium bowl, mash avocados with lemon juice and salt.

3 Crack eggs and gently drop into boiling water. Cook 4 to 6 minutes, or until firm on the outside.

4 Meanwhile, toast bread and spread avocado mixture on toast. Using a slotted spoon, remove eggs from water and place 1 on each slice of toast. Sprinkle with black pepper and drizzle with sriracha. Serve immediately.

Did You Know? *Adding white vinegar to the water for poaching eggs helps make the egg whites firm up even faster, preventing them from spreading out in the water. Also, we've found that the fresher the egg, the better it works for poaching, since the egg white tends to stay more "tightly" together.*

All-In-One Breakfast Bowl

We did it! We got all of your savory breakfast favorites into one dish and it didn't take us more than a half hour. Now, you can enjoy your bacon, eggs, veggies, and potatoes without having to make any sacrifices. So, grab a bowl and enjoy your morning feast!

Serves 4

Ingredients

- 8 slices bacon
- 4 tablespoons butter
- ¾ cup chopped onion
- ½ cup chopped red or green bell pepper
- 2 cups refrigerated diced potatoes (see note)
- 6 eggs
- 2 tablespoons milk
- ½ teaspoon salt
- ¼ teaspoon black pepper

Preparation

1 Preheat oven to 375 degrees F. Place bacon on baking sheet. Cook 15 to 20 minutes, or until crispy.

2 Meanwhile, in a large skillet over medium-high heat, melt butter. Add onion and bell pepper and sauté 5 minutes. Add potatoes and sauté 10 minutes, or until mixture starts to brown.

3 In a medium bowl, beat eggs with milk, salt, and pepper. Pour into skillet with potato mixture and cook 3 to 4 minutes or until eggs are set, stirring occasionally. Divide egg mixture into bowls, top with bacon, and serve.

Super Time Saver: *By using store-bought, refrigerated, diced potatoes we save on prep time. You can even use frozen seasoning blend (chopped onions and peppers) instead of chopping your own. It's easy shortcuts like these that are lifesavers on busy mornings!*

Mediterranean Breakfast Wrap

Tired of having the same ol' breakfast burrito over and over again? So are we! That's why we came up with this Mediterranean-inspired version that's made with some of your favorite fresh flavors. These are even great to make ahead and eat on-the-go, especially when you've got to rush out the door!

Serves 4

Ingredients

5 eggs

2 tablespoons milk

½ teaspoon salt

¼ teaspoon black pepper

2 tablespoons butter

¾ cup cooked pork sausage crumbles

2 tablespoons sliced black olives

1 cup fresh spinach

4 (10-inch) spinach flour tortillas

¼ cup crumbled feta cheese

Preparation

1 Preheat oven to 375 degrees F.

2 In a medium bowl, beat eggs, milk, salt, and pepper until well combined.

3 In a large skillet over medium heat, melt butter. Sauté sausage crumbles 4 to 5 minutes, or until browned. Add egg mixture, olives, and spinach to skillet and cook 3 to 5 minutes, or until eggs are scrambled and spinach is wilted.

4 Spoon egg mixture evenly onto center of tortillas and sprinkle evenly with feta cheese. Fold bottom of tortilla up over the mixture. Fold the left side over, then the right side, and roll up forming a cylinder shape. Place each on a piece of aluminum foil and roll up, securing the ends.

5 Bake 6 to 8 minutes, or until warmed through. Serve immediately.

Serving Suggestion: *We like to enjoy these with a little tzatziki sauce on the side for dipping! If you'd like to make your own, in a large bowl, combine 2 large cucumbers which you've peeled, seeded, and grated, with 2 cups sour cream, 2 teaspoons lemon juice, 4 tablespoons chopped fresh dill, and salt and pepper to taste. Keep any leftover sauce in the refrigerator.*

Broccoli 'n' Ham Mini Quiches

These crustless mini quiches are just what you need when you want something quick for the kids as they head out the door or you've got company coming over for brunch and you don't have a lot of time to prepare. Although they're small in size, they're big on flavor—loaded with lots of cheese, broccoli, and ham. They're so simple and satisfying, it's hard not to love them.

Makes 12

Ingredients

¾ cup pancake and baking mix

1 teaspoon onion powder

¼ teaspoon salt

¼ teaspoon black pepper

1 cup shredded cheddar cheese

½ cup diced ham

1-½ cups frozen broccoli florets, thawed and coarsely chopped

1-¼ cups half-and-half

3 eggs, beaten

Preparation

1 Preheat oven to 400 degrees F. Coat a 12-cup muffin tin with cooking spray.

2 In a large bowl, combine baking mix, onion powder, salt, and pepper; mix well. Stir in cheese, ham, and broccoli. Add half-and-half and eggs; mix well. Pour evenly into muffin cups.

3 Bake 20 to 22 minutes, or until toothpick comes out clean. Let cool 5 minutes, then serve.

Test Kitchen Tip: *These can be made ahead of time and frozen. When you're ready to eat them, simply pop them into the microwave or toaster oven until heated through.*

Brown Sugar Bacon Buttermilk Waffles

If you've been neglecting your waffle iron, we're about to reunite you the tastiest way we know how. It involves the three B's: bacon, buttermilk, and brown sugar. This trio of ingredients makes for a winning combination, resulting in waffles that are just the perfect amount of tangy, sweet, and salty. One bite and you'll never part again.

Makes 5 large waffles

Ingredients

2 cups pancake mix

3 tablespoons light brown sugar

1-½ cups buttermilk

2 tablespoons vegetable oil

1 egg

1 teaspoon vanilla extract

½ cup ready-to-serve bacon pieces

Preparation

1 Preheat an electric waffle iron; coat with cooking spray.

2 In a large bowl, whisk pancake mix, brown sugar, buttermilk, oil, egg, and vanilla until thoroughly combined. Stir in bacon.

3 Using a ½-cup measure, pour batter onto bottom of waffle iron. (Waffle makers vary in size, so you may need a little more or less batter depending on the size of your waffle maker. Your manual will suggest the right amount.) Close lid and cook 1-½ to 2 minutes, or until golden. Using a fork, carefully remove waffle to a plate. Repeat with remaining batter. Serve immediately.

Serving Suggestion: *For a truly mouthwatering presentation, we like to top our waffles with a generous drizzle of maple syrup and lots of extra bacon pieces.*

Lusciously Lemony Ricotta Pancakes

Lemon and ricotta make the perfect pair, which is why we put the two together in this easy and satisfying pancake recipe. The ricotta makes these pancakes extra-moist and fluffy while the lemon zest adds a refreshing tanginess. All in all, these pancakes have everything you've been looking for.

Makes about 12

Ingredients

1 cup ricotta cheese

2 eggs, separated

¾ cup milk

Zest of 1 lemon

1 cup all-purpose flour

1 teaspoon baking powder

2 tablespoons sugar

¼ teaspoon salt

Preparation

1 In a medium bowl, combine ricotta cheese, egg yolks, milk, and lemon zest; mix well.

2 In a large bowl, whisk flour, baking powder, sugar, and salt; stir in ricotta mixture until combined. (This is our homemade pancake batter!)

3 In a small bowl, whisk egg whites until frothy; fold into pancake batter.

4 Coat a griddle or skillet with cooking spray, then heat over medium-low heat. Pour 1/3 cup batter onto griddle for each pancake. When bubbles form on top, flip pancakes and cook 1 to 2 minutes, or until golden. Repeat with remaining batter. Serve immediately.

Finishing Touch: *Fresh blueberries go great with these pancakes. And don't forget to set out the maple syrup, so everyone can drizzle or pour as they please!*

Bumbleberry
Dutch Pancake

The good news is, this one's a no-flipper. What does that mean? It means that this is the recipe you need when you're craving pancakes, but don't want to stand in front of the stove flipping one pancake after another. As a bonus, this pancake is also a showstopper, since it magically puffs up in the oven!

Serves 4

Ingredients

1-½ cups sliced fresh strawberries

¾ cup fresh blueberries

¾ cup fresh raspberries

2 tablespoons sugar

1 tablespoon butter, melted

2 eggs

¼ cup all-purpose flour

¼ cup milk

¼ teaspoon salt

1 cup whipped topping

Preparation

1 Preheat oven to 425 degrees F.

2 In a medium bowl, combine strawberries, blueberries, raspberries, and sugar; mix well and set aside.

3 Coat pie plate with melted butter.

4 In a medium bowl, with an electric mixer, mix eggs, flour, milk, and salt until smooth. Pour into pie plate.

5 Bake 15 to 18 minutes, or until puffy and golden. Spoon berry mixture into pancake, dollop with whipped topping, and serve immediately.

Did You Know? *There's no such thing as a "bumbleberry." However, the combo of three or more types of berries is often referred to as bumbleberries. So, feel free to fill your pancake with any combination of your favorite berries. After all, anything goes in this family-sized pancake!*

Caramel Pecan Stuffed French Toast

You'll be smacking your lips after you get a taste of this French toast! It's the gooiest, sweetest, and most satisfying "dessert for breakfast." Yes, we said dessert for breakfast. A generous drizzle of caramel and a sprinkle of pecans really gives it the perfect finishing touch.

Serves 4

Ingredients

4 ounces cream cheese, softened

2 tablespoons light brown sugar

½ teaspoon ground cinnamon

8 slices white bread

2 eggs

⅓ cup half-and-half

2 tablespoons granulated sugar

4 tablespoons butter

½ cup caramel sauce

¼ cup pecan halves

Preparation

1 In a small bowl, combine cream cheese, brown sugar and cinnamon; mix well. Spread evenly over 4 bread slices. Top with remaining bread slices.

2 In a shallow bowl, whisk eggs, half-and-half, and granulated sugar until well combined.

3 In a large skillet over medium heat, melt two tablespoons butter.

4 Dip each sandwich into egg mixture, completely coating both sides. Cook 2 sandwiches at a time 1 to 2 minutes per side, or until golden. Melt remaining 2 tablespoons butter in skillet and cook remaining 2 sandwiches. Drizzle with caramel sauce and top with pecans.

Chocolate-Hazelnut & Banana French Toast Bake

For the record, chocolate-hazelnut spread goes well with everything; it's almost a fact. Here, we've used it to make an incredible breakfast that looks and tastes like a cross between French toast and bread pudding. The minute you take this out of the oven, your family is going to be ready and waiting at the table.

Serves 6

Ingredients

3 ripe bananas

4 eggs

¾ cup milk

½ stick butter, melted

3 tablespoons sugar

1 teaspoon vanilla extract

1 (12-ounce) loaf French bread, cut into 1-inch pieces

½ cup chocolate-hazelnut spread, slightly warmed

Preparation

1 Preheat oven to 400 degrees F. Coat a 9- x 13-inch baking dish with cooking spray.

2 In a large bowl, mash bananas with a fork, then add the eggs, milk, butter, sugar, and vanilla; mix well. Add bread and toss until completely coated. Pour into baking dish.

3 Bake 18 to 20 minutes, or until set and golden. Drizzle chocolate-hazelnut spread over top, cut into squares, and serve.

Test Kitchen Tip: *If your bananas aren't ripe, you can always place them in a toaster oven, preheated to 250 degrees F, for about 30 minutes or until the skins turn black. Then, peel them and get ready for the sweetest bananas you've ever tasted.*

Old-World
Kielbasa Potato Hash

When you're craving something extra-hearty for breakfast or "brinner" (that's "breakfast for dinner"!), you've got to make this hash. Because it's made with plenty of potatoes and lots of kielbasa, you're sure to leave the table feeling full and satisfied. And since we cook everything together with peppers and onions, you can bet it's flavorful!

Serves 6

Ingredients

3 tablespoons vegetable oil

1 (20-ounce) package refrigerated diced potatoes

½ cup chopped onion

½ red bell pepper, chopped

½ green bell pepper, chopped

¾ teaspoon salt

¼ teaspoon black pepper

½ a (16-ounce) package turkey kielbasa, cut into ¼-inch rounds

Preparation

1 In a large skillet over medium-high heat, heat oil; sauté potatoes, onion, bell peppers, salt, and pepper 10 minutes, or until potatoes begin to brown, stirring occasionally.

2 Stir in kielbasa and cook 5 more minutes, or until kielbasa begins to brown.

So Many Options: *Kielbasa, also known as Polish sausage, is available in different varieties in your supermarket. Feel free to use your favorite kind to make this breakfast hash a family favorite. We also like to enjoy this topped with fried or poached eggs.*

Sunshine Smoothie Bowls

These days, smoothies are being eaten with a spoon almost as often as they're being slurped up through a straw. Smoothie bowls are really popular and it's easy to see why - just check out those toppings! These bright and cheery bowls are sure to bring some extra sunshine to your morning.

Serves 2

Ingredients

1 banana

½ cup strawberries, hulled

1 mango, peeled and pit removed

1-½ cups ice cubes

½ cup vanilla yogurt

¼ cup milk

Assorted fruit, nuts and granola for topping

1 tablespoon honey

Preparation

1 In a blender, combine all ingredients, except toppings and honey. Blend until mixture is smooth and thick.

2 Pour into 2 cereal bowls.

3 Arrange cut fruit, nuts, or granola over smoothie as desired. Drizzle with honey and serve.

So Many Options: *What makes this recipe so much fun is how easy it is to customize! If you're someone who likes a smoothie bowl with lots of crunch, then go on and add more nuts and granola. If you're craving tropical flavors, then sprinkle on some toasted coconut and top with plenty of pineapple and mango chunks. These are just a couple of our favorite ideas to get you started – it's up to you to make it your own!*

Homemade Almond Cheese Danish

Over the years, we've learned that one of your favorite pastries is the classic cheese Danish. We've also learned that you love when we come up with ways to change it up (just a little bit!), so you can try something new. That's what we've done with this recipe. By adding some crunchy almonds and almond flavoring, we've come up with another winning version for you to add to your breakfast or brunch menu.

Serves 15

Ingredients

¼ cup sliced almonds

1 cup sugar, divided

½ teaspoon ground cinnamon

2 (8-ounce) cans refrigerated crescent rolls, divided

12 ounces cream cheese, softened (see Tip)

1 teaspoon almond extract

2 tablespoons butter, melted

Preparation

1 Preheat oven to 375 degrees F. In a small bowl, combine almonds, ¼ cup sugar, and the cinnamon; set aside.

2 Unroll 1 can of crescent dough and press into bottom of an ungreased 9- x 13-inch baking dish, pressing seams together.

3 In a large bowl, combine cream cheese, the remaining ¾ cup sugar, and the almond extract; mix well.

4 Carefully spread cream cheese mixture over dough. Unroll remaining can of dough and place over cream cheese mixture. Brush butter evenly over dough and sprinkle with nut mixture.

5 Bake 20 to 25 minutes, or until golden brown. Let cool before cutting.

Test Kitchen Tip: *To soften the cream cheese in a flash, just place it, unwrapped, on a microwave-safe plate, and microwave for 15 to 20 seconds. (Be careful not to overdo it!)*

Speedy Soups & Sandwiches

Ooey-Gooey Chicken Parm Soup

Leave them speechless by serving up this extra-cheesy chicken soup for dinner. We put lots of cheese into each bowl to make sure there's plenty of ooey-gooey-yummy in every spoonful. And when you use your favorite spaghetti sauce and croutons, you can be sure your family will add this one to their list of "Best Italian Dinners Ever."

Serves 4

Ingredients

3 cups chicken broth

2 cups spaghetti sauce

½ teaspoon Italian seasoning

3 boneless, skinless chicken breasts, cut into ½-inch chunks

4 teaspoons grated Parmesan cheese

1 cup seasoned croutons

4 slices mozzarella cheese

Preparation

1 Preheat oven to 425 degrees F.

2 In a large soup pot over medium-high heat, combine chicken broth, spaghetti sauce, and Italian seasoning. Bring to a boil, add chicken, and cook 5 to 7 minutes, or until chicken is no longer pink.

3 Ladle soup into 4 (2-cup) ovenproof bowls or soup crocks and place on baking sheet. Top each bowl with a teaspoon of Parmesan cheese, ¼ cup croutons, and a slice of mozzarella cheese.

4 Bake 5 to 7 minutes, or until cheese is melted. Serve immediately.

Fancy-Schmancy Steak House Soup

Here's a soup for all the meat and potato lovers out there. Big chunks of potato, plentiful slices of juicy-cooked steak, and savory mushrooms, all swimming in a rich broth, make this soup a mouthwatering favorite. Every spoonful is destined to deliver the taste of your favorite steak house, while still providing all the comfort of a soup bowl.

Serves 6

Ingredients

2 baking potatoes, pricked with a fork

3 tablespoons butter

1 (8-ounce) strip steak, well trimmed

½ pound fresh mushrooms, sliced

2 (10.5-ounce) cans condensed French onion soup

2 cups water

½ teaspoon black pepper

Preparation

1 Microwave potatoes on high 6 to 7 minutes, or until fork tender.

2 Meanwhile, in a soup pot over high heat, melt butter; cook steak and mushrooms 5 to 6 minutes, or until steak is medium rare. Remove steak to a cutting board.

3 Add remaining ingredients to soup pot and bring to a boil. Cut steak into thin slices, cut potatoes into ½-inch chunks, and return both to soup pot. Cook 3 to 5 minutes, or until heated through. Serve immediately.

Test Kitchen Tip: *For the tastiest results, make sure the steak is only heated in the broth for a few minutes. So, if you're planning on putting some soup away for tomorrow or the next day, keep the steak strips separate, until right before serving the soup.*

In-a-Wink
Chicken Tortilla Soup

Instead of cutting up tons of veggies and measuring out spices, we figured out an easier way to add Southwestern flavor to this tortilla soup. The trick—use salsa! Add some chicken and a few other Tex-Mex must-haves, like tortilla strips and fresh cilantro, and you've got yourself a new family favorite.

Serves 6

Ingredients

8 cups chicken broth

1 (16-ounce) jar salsa

2 boneless, skinless chicken breasts, cut into ½-inch chunks

½ cup sliced black olives

2 tablespoons chopped fresh cilantro

4 (6-inch) flour tortillas, cut into ¼- x 3-inch strips

½ cup finely shredded cheddar cheese

Preparation

1 In a soup pot over medium-high heat, bring chicken broth and salsa to a boil. Add chicken and cook 5 minutes, or until no pink remains in the chicken.

2 Stir in olives, cilantro, and tortilla strips and cook 2 minutes, or until heated through.

3 Sprinkle each bowl with a little cheese just before serving.

Simply Delicious Black Bean Soup

As you might've guessed, it doesn't take a lot to make this black bean soup taste delicious. With some basic veggies and a few pantry staples, you can whip up this soup. In no time at all, it's restaurant-special. By the way, this one is real hearty, so make sure you leave enough room in your belly to fill up!

Serves 4

Ingredients

2 (15-ounce) cans black beans, undrained, divided

1 tablespoon olive oil

1 small onion, finely chopped

2 cloves garlic, minced

1-¾ cups chicken broth

1 cup salsa

1 teaspoon ground cumin

Preparation

1 In a blender, puree one can of black beans with its liquid until smooth; set aside.

2 In a medium saucepan over medium heat, heat oil until hot, but not smoking. Sauté onion 4 to 5 minutes, or until soft. Stir in garlic.

3 Add pureed beans to the onions along with the remaining can of undrained beans. Add the chicken broth, salsa, and cumin; mix well.

4 Heat over medium-low heat 10 minutes, or until hot.

Serving Suggestion: *Garnish with a dollop of sour cream and a sprinkle of cilantro. It'll add an extra dose of fancy to each bowl.*

Bread Bowl Shrimp Bisque

Serving soup in bread bowls is an easy way to turn your soup course into a main course (it's also a great way to impress anyone!). When you serve our velvety shrimp bisque in individual, crusty rolls, get ready to rake in the compliments. Plus, once the soup's gone, you get to enjoy all the soup-soaked goodness from the edible bowl.

Serves 4

Ingredients

- 3 tablespoons butter
- 2 tablespoons minced onion
- 3 tablespoons all-purpose flour
- 1 quart half-and-half
- ½ cup cocktail sherry
- 1 teaspoon seafood seasoning
- ½ teaspoon salt
- ¼ teaspoon paprika
- 2 cups raw shrimp, peeled, deveined, and chopped
- 4 kaiser rolls

Preparation

1 In a soup pot over medium heat, melt butter. Sauté onion 3 minutes, or until tender. Add flour, stirring until blended. Cook 1 minute, stirring constantly. Gradually add half-and-half, sherry, seafood seasoning, salt, and paprika; bring just to a simmer.

2 Cook, uncovered, 5 minutes, or until slightly thickened, stirring occasionally (do not boil!). Stir in shrimp and cook 5 to 7 minutes, or until pink.

3 Using a steak knife, cut a circle out of the top of each roll and hollow out the inside, leaving a ½-inch border. Ladle soup into rolls and serve immediately.

Test Kitchen Tip: *Don't waste the inner bread! You can serve it alongside each bread bowl for dipping into the soup or save it and use it to make croutons or bread crumbs. Oh, and before you serve each bowl, we suggest topping them with a couple sprigs of fresh thyme; it'll add a pop of color!*

Weeknight Wedding Soup

This popular Italian-American soup is full of greens and mini meatballs. The marriage of the two ingredients is what gives this soup its name, but it's all the flavors in each bowl that really make it a dinnertime favorite. Be sure to serve it with something dunkable, so they can sop up all the goodness!

Serves 6

Ingredients

8 cups chicken broth

3 cups cocktail-sized frozen meatballs

½ cup orzo

4 cups freshly chopped escarole or spinach

½ cup grated Parmesan cheese, plus extra for garnish

¼ teaspoon black pepper

Preparation

1 In a soup pot over medium-high heat, bring broth to a boil. Add meatballs and orzo, and cook 8 to 10 minutes, or until orzo is tender. Stir in escarole, ½ cup Parmesan cheese, and black pepper, and cook 2 more minutes.

2 Serve with additional Parmesan cheese sprinkled on top.

So Many Options: *When it comes to the meatballs, feel free to use anything from traditional Italian meatballs to low-fat turkey ones. Just make sure you use mini or cocktail-sized ones; this way they'll fit perfectly on your spoon.*

Just-Like-Mom's Chicken & Dumplings

Many of us have warm memories of watching Mom put together her homemade chicken and dumplings. We'd watch her take out all the ingredients to form the dumpling dough, then try to be patient as she'd knead, cut, and prepare the dumplings for cooking. While we loved her homemade version, we realized it would be great to have a semi-homemade way to make it for busy days. Now, we can enjoy this childhood favorite at a moment's notice.

Serves 6

Ingredients

2 tablespoons butter

2 celery stalks, thinly sliced

2 carrots, thinly sliced

8 cups chicken broth

½ teaspoon poultry seasoning

¼ teaspoon black pepper

3 cups pulled or chopped rotisserie chicken

1 (10.2-ounce) package refrigerated biscuits, each biscuit cut into 8 pieces

Preparation

1 In a soup pot over medium-high heat, melt butter. Add celery and carrots and sauté 4 minutes, or until tender. Stir in broth, poultry seasoning, and pepper; bring to a boil. Stir in chicken.

2 Drop biscuit pieces, one at a time, into boiling mixture. Cover, reduce heat to low, and simmer 8 to 10 minutes, or until dumplings are cooked through, stirring occasionally.

Super Time Saver: *If you buy a rotisserie chicken, it's a lot faster to pull the meat from the frame while it's still warm. So, when you get it home from the market and it's still warm, that's the time to do it.*

Asian Veggies & Noodle Soup

Your nose will fall in love with this soup before your taste buds do. Aromatics like ginger and garlic add so much flavor and depth to each bowl. And since this one is meat-free and features oodles of noodles (along with bok choy and mushrooms), you can bet it's a vegetarian favorite.

Serves 5

Ingredients

4 cups water

4 ounces Asian-style rice noodles

4 cups vegetable broth

1 teaspoon thinly sliced fresh ginger root

2 cloves garlic, minced

1 tablespoon soy sauce

¼ teaspoon salt

¼ teaspoon black pepper

2 cups sliced mushrooms

2-½ cups sliced bok choy

Preparation

1 In a medium saucepan over high heat, bring water to a boil. Stir in rice noodles, remove from heat, and let sit 10 minutes, or until softened; drain.

2 Meanwhile, in a soup pot over medium-high heat, combine vegetable broth, ginger, and garlic and bring to a boil. Stir in soy sauce, salt, and pepper. Add mushrooms and cook 5 minutes, or until mushrooms are soft. Stir in bok choy and rice noodles, and simmer 2 minutes. Serve immediately.

So Many Options: *You can use any of your favorite mushrooms in this soup, including shiitake, oyster, cremini, or even white button mushrooms. And if you like a little crunch with your soup, we suggest serving it with a side of wonton strips (located next to the other salad toppings in your supermarket).*

Two-Bean Turkey Chili

We're not fans of bland and boring chili. When we do chili, we want it to knock your socks off with how good it is. So, we put all the good stuff in this one. This flavor-packed chili is brimming with veggies, two kinds of beans, and plenty of meaty goodness. You definitely won't leave the table hungry after this one.

Serves 6

Ingredients

1 tablespoon olive oil

1 onion, chopped

1 green bell pepper, chopped

1 teaspoon chopped garlic

1 pound ground turkey breast

1 (15.3-ounce) can black-eyed peas, rinsed and drained

1 (15-ounce) can red kidney beans, undrained

3 (14-½-ounce) cans diced tomatoes, undrained

2 tablespoons chili powder

1 teaspoon ground cumin

1 teaspoon salt

½ teaspoon black pepper

Preparation

1 In a large pot over medium-high heat, heat oil until hot, but not smoking. Add onion, bell pepper, and garlic, and cook 3 minutes. Add turkey and cook 5 minutes, or until no pink remains in turkey, stirring occasionally to break it up.

2 Add remaining ingredients. Bring to a boil, stirring occasionally. Reduce heat to low, cover, and simmer 20 minutes.

Serving Suggestion: *Break out the bread for this one, 'cause they're going to want to leave their bowls clean.*

Mac & Cheese Grilled Cheese

Did you notice that we got "cheese" into the name of this recipe twice? That's because this sandwich features double the cheesiness! You see, we weren't satisfied with just a regular grilled cheese sandwich. We wanted to make something that would drop the jaws of even the most fanatic of cheese lovers. It turns out two cheesy classics do make a right.

Serves 2

Ingredients

1 (12-ounce) package frozen macaroni and cheese

4 slices sour dough bread

4 slices cheddar cheese

2 tablespoons butter, softened

Preparation

1 Microwave macaroni and cheese according to package directions.

2 Place 2 slices of bread on counter. Place a slice of Cheddar on each and top with a scoop of macaroni and cheese in center. Top with remaining cheese slices and bread, pressing down lightly, so the macaroni spreads to the edges (don't worry if a little oozes out!). Spread half the butter on top of sandwiches.

3 In a large skillet over medium-low heat, place sandwiches butter-side down and spread remaining butter on top of bread. Cook sandwiches 1 to 2 minutes on each side, turning halfway through, until it's golden on both sides and cheese is melted.

Hot 'n' Hearty
Roast Beef Melt

A simple cream cheese-horseradish spread on crusty bread forms the base of this delectable sandwich. Pile on the layers of roast beef, red peppers, and buttery-tasting Havarti cheese and you're on your way to perfection. All that's left is the seasoning and the statement-making onion rings. You might want to step back and admire your handiwork before you take your first bite.

Serves 6

Ingredients

1 (8-ounce) package cream cheese, softened

2 tablespoons prepared horseradish, drained

1 (16-ounce) ciabatta or French bread

1 pound thinly sliced deli roast beef

1 (12-ounce) jar roasted red pepper strips, drained and patted dry, sliced into ¼-inch strips

8 slices Havarti cheese

2 teaspoons Montreal steak seasoning

16 frozen onion rings

Preparation

1 Preheat oven to 425 degrees F. Coat a baking sheet with cooking spray.

2 In a medium bowl, mix cream cheese and horseradish until creamy.

3 Cut bread in half, lengthwise, and spread both halves with cream cheese spread. Loosely pile roast beef over cheese spread, then top evenly with red pepper strips and cheese slices. Sprinkle with seasoning, place onion rings on top, and place on baking sheet.

4 Bake 20 minutes, or until heated through and onion rings are golden.

Test Kitchen Tip: *This makes for a great game day sandwich. Cut into slices, break out the beer mugs, and watch as they go to town on this bad boy!*

Chick 'n' Waffle Sandwiches

A meal like this doesn't really need a special introduction, but we're going to introduce you anyway. Meet our extra-crunchy, super-juicy, buttermilk-fried chicken, topped with two slices of crispy bacon, and sandwiched between two waffles that've been drizzled with sweet maple syrup. Now that you've met, you're going to want no interruptions as you chew your way through each bite.

Serves 4

Ingredients

8 slices bacon

1 cup all-purpose flour

1-½ teaspoons paprika

1 teaspoon seafood seasoning

1 teaspoon garlic powder

½ teaspoon salt

1 teaspoon black pepper

1 cup buttermilk

1-½ cups vegetable oil

8 chicken tenders

8 frozen waffles, toasted according to package directions

Syrup for drizzling

Preparation

1. Preheat oven to 400 degrees F.

2. Place bacon on baking sheet and cook 15 minutes, or until crispy. Transfer to a paper towel-lined platter to drain.

3. Meanwhile, in a shallow dish, combine flour, paprika, seafood seasoning, garlic powder, salt, and pepper; mix well. Place buttermilk in another shallow dish.

4. In a large deep skillet over medium heat, heat oil until hot but not smoking. Dip chicken tenders in buttermilk, then in flour mixture, coating evenly on all sides. Fry chicken 8 to 10 minutes, or until golden and no pink remains, turning once during cooking. Drain on a paper towel-lined platter.

5. Place 2 chicken tenders on each of 4 waffles. Top each with 2 slices bacon, drizzle with syrup, and top with remaining waffles.

Test Kitchen Tip: *All that juicy chicken and syrupy goodness makes this sandwich a little messy, so we recommend eating with a fork...and lots of napkins. By the way, since this sandwich features waffles and fried chicken, it's just as good for breakfast as it is for lunch or dinner.*

Oven-Baked Cuban Sliders

The "Cubano" is one of America's favorite sandwiches, up there with the Philly Cheesesteak, the Reuben, and the BLT. For an authentic-tasting version, you've got to make sure there's plenty of pickles, pork, ham, cheese, and yellow mustard. Oh, and it's always got to be served toasty (that's a widely accepted rule). These Cuban Sliders are perfect for bringing along to a potluck and sharing with friends. Maybe someone else can be in charge of the mojitos?

Serves 6

Ingredients

1 (12-count) package Hawaiian sweet dinner rolls

¼ cup yellow mustard, divided

½ pound thinly sliced deli ham

½ pound thinly sliced deli pork

¾ cup pickle chips

8 slices Swiss cheese

2 tablespoons melted butter

Preparation

1 Preheat oven to 400 degrees F.

2 Slice entire package of rolls in half horizontally, keeping bottom half of rolls together and top halves of rolls together; place bottom halves in a 9- x 13-inch baking dish. Spread cut side of both top and bottom halves evenly with mustard. Layer evenly with ham, pork, pickles, and cheese, and place top half of buns over cheese. Brush with butter, then cover with aluminum foil.

3 Bake 15 to 20 minutes, or until heated through. Remove from oven and cut between the rolls to make individual sliders.

Serving Suggestion: *Traditionally, a Cuban sandwich might be served with a side of "tostones" (twice-fried plantains), but if you're not up to frying, we suggest serving with a side of plantain chips. These can be found in many supermarkets across the country, in the chip aisle or in the ethnic food aisle.*

Everything-in-It Chicken Burritos

Lots of restaurants offer a "build your own burrito" option where you walk down a line and choose the kinds of fillings you want. If you're like most of us in the Test Kitchen, you like it all—rice, beans, chicken, corn, salsa...just to name a few. Since making a burrito with everything you love is so easy to do, we're asking that you step out of line and give it a try at home. You can even make these ahead of time for a busy day lunch.

Serves 3

Ingredients

1 cup water

2 tablespoons lime juice

1 cup instant rice

2 tablespoons chopped fresh cilantro

1 (15-ounce) can black beans, rinsed and drained

2 cups diced rotisserie or pre-cooked chicken

1 teaspoon ground cumin

3 (10-inch) flour tortillas

½ cup salsa, divided

¾ cup corn, divided

½ cup shredded Colby-Jack cheese

Preparation

1 Preheat oven to 400 degrees F. Cut 3 (12- x 12-inch) pieces aluminum foil.

2 In a small saucepan over high heat, combine water, lime juice, and rice; bring to a boil, cover, remove from heat, and let sit 5 minutes, or until water is absorbed and rice is fluffy. Stir in cilantro and black beans.

3 In a medium bowl, combine chicken and cumin; mix well. Spoon rice mixture evenly down center of each tortilla. Top with chicken, salsa, corn, and cheese. Fold up bottom of tortilla over mixture. Fold the left side in, then the right side, and roll up forming a cylinder shape. Place burritos seam side down on foil pieces and roll up. Place on baking sheet.

4 Bake 5 to 7 minutes, or until warmed through.

Couch Potato Burger

If today's plans include sitting on your couch and catching up on your favorite TV shows, then we've got the perfect burger to keep you company (though you might make it disappear before you get to the second episode). We've topped this burger not only with a mountain of curly fries, but with lots of melty Swiss which takes it over the top. Keep the napkins close by; things might get a little messy!

Serves 4

Ingredients

2 cups frozen curly fries

1 pound ground beef

½ teaspoon salt

¼ teaspoon black pepper

¼ pound deli pastrami, coarsely chopped

4 slices Swiss cheese

4 hamburger buns

¼ cup Russian dressing

Preparation

1 Preheat oven to 425 degrees F. Coat a baking sheet with cooking spray.

2 Place fries on baking sheet and bake 20 minutes, or until crispy.

3 Meanwhile, in a large bowl, combine beef, salt, pepper, and pastrami; mix well. Form mixture into 4 patties.

4 In a large skillet or grill pan over medium heat, cook burgers 5 to 6 minutes per side, or until desired doneness. Top each with a slice of cheese and heat 1 minute, or until cheese is slightly melted. Place each burger on a bun, top with dressing and fries, and serve.

Test Kitchen Tip: *If you want to go topless, feel free to leave off the top of the burger and get your grub on!*

Unbeatable Veggie Burgers

Not all veggie burgers are cut from the same cloth. Some of them can be really tasteless and dry, causing beef-lovers to declare victory. But, if you've tried a veggie burger made from real veggies (like ours!), then you know that they can be a tasty alternative to the meaty versions. Make these for your next weeknight dinner and you'll impress everyone.

Makes 4

Ingredients

1 (15-ounce) can black beans, rinsed and drained, divided

2 cups (6 ounces) chopped portabella mushrooms

1 cup chopped fresh broccoli florets

¾ cup frozen corn, thawed

¼ cup minced red onion

1 teaspoon garlic powder

1 teaspoon salt

¼ teaspoon black pepper

2 eggs, beaten

1 tablespoon Worcestershire sauce

1 cup Italian bread crumbs

¼ cup grated Parmesan cheese

1 tablespoon olive oil

4 hamburger buns

Preparation

1 In a large bowl, mash 1 cup black beans. Add remaining whole black beans, the mushrooms, broccoli, corn, onion, garlic powder, salt, and pepper; mix well. Add eggs, Worcestershire sauce, bread crumbs, and Parmesan cheese; mix just until combined. Form mixture into 4 patties.

2 Heat a large skillet over medium heat. Heat oil until hot, but not smoking, and cook burgers 4 to 5 minutes per side, or until golden brown and heated through. Place each burger on a bun and serve.

Serving Suggestion: *Make these your own by adding your favorite toppings. We especially like to serve these with a little fresh salsa, guacamole and curly leaf lettuce.*

Turkey Burgers with Caramelized Onions

Your family is going to "gobble" up these burgers! To end up with these juicy, cheesy, and flavor-packed turkey burgers, we start off with perfectly seasoned patties. Then, we top each one with melty Muenster cheese and a generous amount of tender, sweet onions. Add a little honey mustard for an extra dose of sweet and tangy, and you're ready to rock and roll.

Serves 4

Ingredients

2 tablespoons vegetable oil

1 large sweet onion, thinly sliced

1 tablespoon sugar

1 teaspoon salt, divided

1-¼ pounds ground turkey

¼ cup Italian breadcrumbs

1 egg white

1 teaspoon Worcestershire sauce

¼ teaspoon black pepper

4 slices Muenster cheese

4 hamburger buns

¼ cup honey mustard dressing

Preparation

1 In a large skillet over medium-high heat, heat oil until hot, but not smoking. Sauté onions with sugar and ½ teaspoon salt for 12 to 15 minutes, or until golden brown, stirring occasionally.

2 Meanwhile, in a large bowl, combine turkey, breadcrumbs, egg white, Worcestershire sauce, pepper, and remaining ½ teaspoon salt; mix well. Form mixture into 4 patties.

3 In a grill pan or skillet over medium heat, cook burgers 8 to 12 minutes, or until no pink remains, turning halfway through. Place a slice of cheese on each burger and cook 1 to 2 more minutes, or until cheese is melted. Place burgers on buns, top with caramelized onions, and drizzle with honey mustard dressing.

Serving Suggestion: *Go all out by adding a thick slice of tomato and some soft, Bibb lettuce. The way we look at it, you can never go wrong with more layers. Open up wide!*

Super Simple Sloppy Dogs

In states like Texas and Michigan, adding chili to a hot dog is 100% acceptable and encouraged. While both states like their "dogs" loaded with lots of beefy goodness, they do differ in the kinds of condiments and additional toppings they use. After sampling a few variations, we came up with our own recipe. We know you'll love this sloppy joe version that's beefy, saucy, and definitely flavor-packed.

Serves 4

Ingredients

½ pound ground beef

1 (8-ounce) can tomato sauce

¼ cup ketchup

2 teaspoons Worcestershire sauce

½ teaspoon hot pepper sauce

2 teaspoons chili powder

½ teaspoon garlic powder

¼ teaspoon black pepper

4 hot dogs

4 hot dog rolls

¼ cup diced onion

Preparation

1 In a large skillet over medium heat, cook beef 5 minutes, or until browned, stirring occasionally to break up. Drain off excess liquid. Add tomato sauce, ketchup, Worcestershire sauce, hot pepper sauce, chili powder, garlic powder, and pepper. Cook 5 minutes, stirring occasionally.

2 Meanwhile, in a grill pan or skillet over medium heat, cook hot dogs 6 to 8 minutes, or until heated through. Place hot dogs on rolls, top with beef mixture and onions, and serve.

Serving Suggestion: *If you're serving these at a picnic or cookout, be sure to set out some chips and pickle spears. They make the perfect go-along!*

Pronto Pleasin' Poultry

Picture Perfect Caprese Chicken

Isn't this chicken pretty as a picture? What we like best about caprese dishes is how well the simple ingredients go together. Fresh mozzarella, tomatoes, and basil, topped with a generous drizzle of balsamic glaze make for a great combo with chicken breasts. Since this one is so pretty, be sure to snap a photo to share with your friends on social media, and tag it #MrFood!

Serves 4

Ingredients

4 boneless, skinless chicken breasts

½ teaspoon salt

¼ teaspoon black pepper

2 tablespoons olive oil

2 tomatoes, thinly sliced

4 slices fresh mozzarella cheese

4 leaves fresh basil

Balsamic glaze for drizzling (see note)

Preparation

1 Sprinkle chicken evenly with salt and pepper.

2 In a large skillet over medium-high heat, heat oil until hot, but not smoking; sauté chicken 8 to 10 minutes, or until no longer pink in center, turning once during cooking. Place 2 tomato slices over each chicken breast, and top each with a slice of cheese. Cover skillet and heat 1 minute.

3 Just before serving, drizzle with balsamic glaze and top with fresh basil.

Test Kitchen Tip: *You can find balsamic glaze near the vinegars in your local market. If you don't see it, just ask. Or, if you prefer, you can make your own by simply reducing about a cup of balsamic vinegar mixed with a couple of tablespoons of brown sugar, and simmering it in a saucepan for about 10 to 15 minutes, until it thickens.*

Build-Your-Own Lettuce Wraps

Here's a fresh spread worth celebrating! The best way to get your family to make healthier choices is to let them do it themselves, which is why build-your-own lettuce wraps is such a great idea. Make sure to include some of their favorite fresh veggies in the spread, so they get even more excited. Oh, and wait till you try our homemade cilantro dressing; it's to die for.

Serves 4

Ingredients

CILANTRO DRESSING

¼ cup sour cream

½ cup mayonnaise

½ cup fresh cilantro

2 teaspoons lime juice

1 jalapeño pepper

¼ teaspoon salt

2 boneless, skinless chicken breasts, pounded to ½-inch thickness

¼ teaspoon salt

¼ teaspoon black pepper

1 tablespoon olive oil

1 tablespoon lime juice

12 Boston Bibb lettuce leaves, separated

¾ cup shredded carrot

¾ cup shredded cucumber

1 avocado, thinly sliced

Preparation

1 In a blender, combine Cilantro Dressing ingredients; blend until smooth and creamy. Refrigerate until ready to use.

2 Sprinkle chicken with salt and pepper. In a large skillet over medium-high heat, heat oil until hot, but not smoking. Add lime juice. Sauté chicken 6 to 8 minutes, or until no longer pink in center. Remove chicken to a cutting board and cut into thin strips.

3 Arrange lettuce leaves on a platter along with chicken, carrot, cucumber, and avocado. Place dressing in a bowl and serve on the side. This way everyone can make their own lettuce wraps to their liking.

Mamma Mia's Chicken Parmigiana

Maybe you have an Italian "mamma" in your life or maybe you just frequent the Italian restaurant down the street called "Mamma Mia's." Either way, you've probably had the chance to taste and fall in love with a chicken parmigiana at least once in your life. With all the crispy, cheesy, sauciness, how could you not? Now, you can share the love with your family any night of the week.

Serves 4

Ingredients

2 eggs

¼ teaspoon salt

¼ teaspoon black pepper

1 cup Italian-flavored breadcrumbs

4 boneless, skinless chicken breasts, pounded to ¼-inch thickness

½ cup olive oil

1-½ cups spaghetti sauce, warmed

2 cups (8 ounces) shredded mozzarella cheese

Grated Parmesan cheese for topping

Preparation

1 In a shallow dish, beat eggs, salt, and pepper. Place breadcrumbs in another shallow dish. Dip each chicken breast into egg mixture, then into breadcrumbs, coating completely; set aside.

2 In a large skillet over medium heat, heat oil until hot, but not smoking. Cook chicken breasts two at a time 4 to 5 minutes per side, or until no longer pink in center and golden brown. Drain on paper towels.

3 Preheat oven to broil. Coat a rimmed baking sheet with cooking spray.

4 Place chicken on baking sheet and spoon spaghetti sauce evenly over each piece. Sprinkle with cheese and broil 4 to 5 minutes, or until the cheese is melted and starts to get golden brown around the edges. Serve topped with grated Parmesan cheese.

Old-Fashioned Skillet-Fried Drumsticks

It seems that fried chicken has been around since the beginning of time, but it's one of those old-fashioned dinners that never really gets old. Who can deny the incredible taste of perfectly seasoned, crispy-coated chicken? We can't, and we're willing to bet your family won't either.

Serves 4

Ingredients

1 cup all-purpose flour

1 teaspoon poultry seasoning

2 teaspoons paprika

2 teaspoons salt

1-½ teaspoons black pepper

8 drumsticks

1 cup buttermilk

2 cups vegetable oil

Preparation

1 In a large bowl, combine flour, poultry seasoning, paprika, salt, and pepper; mix well.

2 Dip drumsticks in buttermilk, then into flour mixture, coating completely.

3 In a large, deep skillet over medium heat, heat oil until hot, but not smoking. Fry drumsticks about 10 minutes per side, or until golden and no pink remains. Drain on a paper towel-lined platter. Serve immediately.

Test Kitchen Tip: *If you have a kitchen thermometer, insert the tip of it into the oil and adjust the heat until the oil reaches a temperature of 350 degrees F, which is the ideal temperature for cooking the chicken on the inside without burning the outside.*

Lightning-Quick Thai Chicken Pasta

Thai food can never be described using just one taste. In fact, the Thai are known for coming up with dishes that mix tastes like sweet, salty, and spicy. We always figured it took a long time to get all those kinds of flavors in one dish, until we decided to give it a try. Our inspired version of Thai chicken pasta comes together lightning-quick and features quite a few different tastes. How many can you name?

Serves 6

Ingredients

1 pound linguine

⅓ cup plus 2 tablespoons sesame oil, divided

1-½ pounds boneless, skinless chicken breasts, cut into 1-inch chunks

1 [12-ounce] package frozen Asian-blend vegetable mixture, thawed

1 cup crunchy peanut butter

⅔ cup heavy cream

¼ cup soy sauce

2 cloves garlic, minced

2 tablespoons white vinegar

1 tablespoon sugar

2 teaspoons ground ginger

1 tablespoon crushed red pepper

Preparation

1 In a soup pot, cook linguine according to package directions; drain, rinse, drain again, and set aside in the colander.

2 Meanwhile, in a large skillet over medium-high heat, heat 2 tablespoons sesame oil. Add chicken and brown 5 minutes. Add vegetables and cook 3 to 4 minutes, or until vegetables are heated through.

3 In a medium bowl, combine peanut butter, cream, soy sauce, garlic, vinegar, sugar, ginger, red pepper, and the remaining ⅓ cup oil; mix well.

4 Return linguine to pot and add peanut butter mixture; toss to coat. Stir in chicken and vegetable mixture. Heat on low 3 to 5 minutes, or until mixture is heated through.

Mix 'n' Match: *The Asian blend of veggies we used consisted of broccoli, carrots, sugar snap peas, and water chestnuts, but any combo of veggies will work.*

In-a-Hurry Company Chicken

Every once in a while, you might have some company drop by for a visit during the week. If they're staying for dinner, this is one dish that's always special. It features a triple-whammy of deliciousness that comes from a homemade syrup blend, a crispy pecan coating, and juicy cooked chicken. Heck, you don't even have to wait for company to come—you can just treat your family to something special!

Serves 4

Ingredients

⅓ cup maple syrup

2 tablespoons mayonnaise

1 tablespoon bourbon (optional)

¾ cup panko breadcrumbs

½ cup finely chopped pecans

1 tablespoon sugar

⅛ teaspoon cayenne pepper

4 boneless, skinless chicken breasts

½ teaspoon salt

Cooking spray

Preparation

1 Preheat oven to 375 degrees F. Coat a baking sheet with cooking spray.

2 In a shallow dish, combine syrup, mayonnaise, and bourbon, if desired; mix well. In another dish, combine breadcrumbs, pecans, sugar, and cayenne pepper; mix well.

3 Lightly sprinkle chicken with salt and dip into syrup mixture. Then, place in the pecan mixture, pressing coating onto chicken until it's coated completely. Place on a baking sheet and lightly spray with cooking spray.

4 Bake 18 to 20 minutes, or until coating is golden and the chicken is no longer pink in center.

Fancy It Up: Right before serving, we like to cut the chicken into thick slices on the diagonal (as shown). It makes it look extra-fancy and only takes a second to do.

South-of-the-Border Chicken Dinner

You don't have to travel south of the border to enjoy all of your favorite Tex-Mex flavors. You can just cook up this zesty chicken dinner, which features all the good stuff like corn, beans, tomatoes, and seasoned chicken chunks. Serve it over rice, throw on a sombrero (optional, of course!) and call your family to the table—olé!

Serves 4

Ingredients

2 cups instant rice

1 tablespoon vegetable oil

3 boneless, skinless chicken breasts, cut into ½-inch cubes

1 (1-ounce) package taco seasoning mix

1 (16-ounce) can black beans, rinsed and drained

1 (14.5-ounce) can diced tomatoes with chilies, undrained

2 cups frozen corn, thawed

½ cup shredded Mexican cheese blend

Preparation

1 Cook rice according to package directions.

2 Meanwhile, in a large skillet over medium-high heat, heat oil until hot, but not smoking. Cook chicken 5 minutes, stirring occasionally. Stir in taco seasoning and cook 3 to 4 more minutes, or until no pink remains in the chicken. Add black beans, tomatoes, and corn. Reduce heat to low and simmer 10 minutes or until everything is heated through.

3 Place chicken mixture over rice, sprinkle with cheese, and enjoy.

Good for You! *Draining and rinsing canned beans helps to reduce the sodium by about 40 percent. That sure is good news for anyone watching their salt intake.*

Mushroom 'n' Herb Chicken Skillet

Here you go; the fanciest chicken dinner you'll ever make without dirtying more than one pan. By bathing chicken breasts in a mouthwatering mushroom sauce and topping them with a flavorful cheese spread, we've pretty much guaranteed that these will disappear in less time than it takes to cook them.

Serves 4

Ingredients

4 boneless, skinless chicken breasts

½ teaspoon salt

¼ teaspoon black pepper

2 tablespoons olive oil

1-½ cups sliced fresh mushrooms

½ cup chopped onion

½ teaspoon dried thyme leaves

¾ cup chicken broth

⅓ cup white wine

¼ cup garlic herb cheese spread

Preparation

1 Sprinkle chicken evenly with salt and pepper.

2 In a large skillet over medium heat, heat oil until hot, but not smoking. Sauté chicken 6 to 8 minutes per side, or until browned and no pink remains in center. Remove chicken to a plate; set aside.

3 In the same skillet, cook mushrooms, onion, and thyme 5 minutes. Add chicken broth and wine to skillet and heat 5 more minutes. Return chicken to skillet, top each breast with 1 tablespoon cheese spread, cover, and heat 2 to 3 minutes, or until cheese is melted. Spoon mushroom sauce over chicken and serve immediately.

Super Time Saver: Instead of softening some cream cheese and mixing in a whole bunch of herbs, we save time by using herb cheese spread. It's little tricks like this that help us get dinner on the table in under 30 minutes!

The Fastest Curried Chicken Ever

Most curries we've come across take about an hour or so of simmering on the stove before they're ready to be eaten, but we don't always have that kind of time (and everyone knows that when the cravings set in, it's hard to wait that long!). So, we worked a little Test Kitchen magic and finally came up with a recipe that's fit for those busy days. This rich-tasting and full-flavored, curried chicken is going to change your world.

Serves 6

Ingredients

2 pounds boneless, skinless chicken breasts, cut into ½-inch cubes

½ teaspoon salt

¼ teaspoon black pepper

2 tablespoons vegetable oil

2 tablespoons curry powder

½ cup chopped onion

3 cloves garlic, minced

1 (14-ounce) can coconut milk

1 (14.5-ounce) can diced tomatoes, undrained

1 cup frozen peas

3 tablespoons sugar

3 cups cooked white rice, warmed

Preparation

1 Sprinkle chicken evenly with salt and pepper.

2 In a large skillet over medium-high heat, heat oil and curry powder until hot, but not smoking. Add chicken, onion, and garlic and cook 5 minutes, stirring occasionally.

3 Reduce heat to medium-low; add coconut milk, tomatoes, peas, and sugar. Cook 15 to 20 minutes, or until sauce has thickened slightly and the chicken is no longer pink in center. Serve over rice.

Test Kitchen Tip: *For the rice, you can quickly make your own in a saucepan or rice cooker, or you can pick up a bag of pre-cooked rice that you only have to warm and serve.*

Piled-High
Pulled Chicken Biscuits

Don't be shy about piling on the pulled chicken! Trust us, if you don't put enough, your family is going to ask for more anyway, so it's better to go big the first time. And since these biscuit sandwiches also include some homemade coleslaw, you don't have to worry about making extra side dishes.

Serves 5

Ingredients

1 (10.2-ounce) can Southern-style refrigerated biscuits

1-½ pounds boneless, skinless chicken thighs

1 large onion, thinly sliced

1-½ cups barbecue sauce

½ cup water

2 tablespoons brown sugar

COLESLAW

½ (16-ounce) package coleslaw mix

1 tablespoon vegetable oil

2 tablespoons apple cider vinegar

2 teaspoons granulated sugar

½ teaspoon salt

¼ teaspoon black pepper

Preparation

1 Cook biscuits according to package directions.

2 Meanwhile, in a large skillet over medium-high heat, cook chicken and onion 10 minutes, or until onion begins to brown. Stir in barbecue sauce, water, and brown sugar; cover and cook 10 minutes, or until no pink remains in the chicken and it's fork tender.

3 While chicken is cooking, in a medium bowl, combine Coleslaw ingredients; mix well and set aside.

4 Remove chicken to a cutting board. Using 2 forks, shred chicken by gently pulling it apart. Return chicken to skillet and stir until evenly coated with sauce. Over medium heat, cook 2 minutes, or until heated through.

5 Split each biscuit in half. Top bottom half with chicken, then pile on the coleslaw and finish with the top of the biscuit.

Did You Know? *Chicken thighs are less lean than chicken breasts, which makes them juicier, more flavorful, and less stringy. They're just what we need for recipes like this!*

Sizzlin' Skillet Chicken Fajitas

When the skillet starts sizzlin', everyone will know something tasty is about to happen (or maybe it's the wonderful smell of sautéed peppers and onions that'll tip them off?). Have someone else set out the family's favorite fajita fixins' like cheese, sour cream, and salsa, and bring out the chicken and veggie filling on a sizzling platter. That way, there'll be lots of "oohs" and "aahs," and everyone can build their fajitas just the way they like them.

Makes 6 fajitas

Ingredients

3 tablespoons vegetable oil, divided

2 large onions, each cut into 8 wedges

2 large bell peppers (1 red and 1 green), cut into ¼-inch strips

½ teaspoon salt

¼ teaspoon black pepper

1 pound boneless, skinless chicken breasts, cut into 1-inch strips

1-½ teaspoons chili powder

1 teaspoon cumin

1 teaspoon garlic powder

2 tablespoons fresh lime juice

6 (8-inch) flour tortillas

Preparation

1 In a large skillet over medium-high heat, heat 2 tablespoons oil until hot, but not smoking. Add onions, bell peppers, salt, and pepper; sauté 10 minutes, or until onions are lightly browned. Place in a bowl and set aside.

2 Heat remaining 1 tablespoon oil; add chicken, chili powder, cumin, and garlic powder. Sauté 5 to 6 minutes, or until chicken is no longer pink.

3 Return vegetables to skillet and cook 3 to 5 minutes or until heated through, stirring occasionally.

4 Pour lime juice over chicken and vegetables; mix well. Divide chicken mixture equally among tortillas and serve.

Chicken Caesar Salad Pizza

What's a "salad pizza" you ask? Well, you can think of it as the most brilliant way to get your family to eat salad or you can think of it as the perfect mash-up of two very tasty dishes (we like to think it's both). By switching out the pizza sauce for Caesar dressing and baking with lots of chicken and mozzarella, before topping with the remaining salad ingredients, we get to enjoy the best of both worlds.

Serves 4

Ingredients

2 boneless, skinless chicken breasts, pounded to ¼-inch thickness

¼ teaspoon salt

⅛ teaspoon black pepper

1 tablespoon olive oil

1 (13.8-ounce) can refrigerated pizza crust dough

¼ cup plus 2 tablespoons Caesar dressing, divided

1 cup shredded mozzarella cheese

2 cups shredded romaine lettuce

2 tablespoons shaved Parmesan cheese

Preparation

1 Preheat oven to 425 degrees F. Coat an 11- x 15-inch baking sheet with cooking spray.

2 Sprinkle chicken evenly with salt and pepper. In a large skillet over medium-high heat, heat oil until hot, but not smoking. Cook chicken 3 to 4 minutes per side, or until no longer pink in center. Cut chicken into thin slices.

3 Unroll pizza dough on baking sheet; using your fingers, press dough to edge of baking sheet. Spread ¼ cup Caesar dressing evenly over dough. Top evenly with chicken and mozzarella. Bake 10 to 12 minutes, or until crust is light golden.

4 Meanwhile, in a medium bowl, toss lettuce with remaining 2 tablespoons Caesar dressing. Top pizza evenly with lettuce and Parmesan cheese, cut into 8 slices, and serve.

So Many Options: If you like anchovies on your Caesar salad, place those on right before serving.

Chicken Sausage Pita Pockets

Just because something is hearty and satisfying doesn't mean it has to make you feel overstuffed. You can fill up on these healthier-for-you pitas that are made with lots of fresh veggies and slices of flavorful chicken sausage. To add even more color to our plates, we like to enjoy these with a serving of vegetable chips.

Serves 4

Ingredients

2 tablespoons olive oil

1 (12-ounce) package fully cooked chicken sausage links, cut into ½-inch slices

1 small onion, thinly sliced

1-½ cups sliced fresh mushrooms

1 teaspoon garlic powder

½ teaspoon salt

¼ teaspoon black pepper

2 tomatoes, cut into chunks

2 tablespoons thinly sliced fresh basil

4 whole pitas, cut in half and warmed

½ cup vinaigrette (see note)

Preparation

1 In a large skillet over medium-high heat, heat oil until hot, but not smoking. Cook sausage and onion 5 to 7 minutes, or until sausage is browned. Add mushrooms, garlic powder, salt, and pepper and cook 5 minutes, or until mushrooms are tender.

2 Stir in tomatoes and basil and spoon evenly into pitas.

3 Drizzle with vinaigrette and serve immediately.

So Many Options: *Go ahead and serve these pitas with your favorite kind of vinaigrette. Then, the next time you make this, try it with a different vinaigrette to change up the flavors in your pita. Maybe go with a Greek vinaigrette one time and a balsamic another time?*

Sticky Sesame Chicken Thighs

Did you know that in many parts of the world sesame seeds are said to bring good luck? On those days when your family could use some extra luck, why not whip up this Asian-inspired dish that's topped with the nutty seeds? While we can't guarantee that you'll suddenly win the lotto or that your kids will pass that test tomorrow, we're pretty sure that these juicy and sticky-sweet chicken thighs will lift everyone's spirits up.

Serves 3

Ingredients

1 cup water

1 cup instant white rice

2 teaspoons vegetable oil

2 pounds boneless, skinless chicken thighs

¼ cup rice wine vinegar

3 tablespoons soy sauce

3 tablespoons honey

3 cloves garlic, minced

½ teaspoon ground ginger

2 scallions, sliced

1 teaspoon sesame seeds

Preparation

1 In a medium saucepan over high heat, bring water to a boil; add rice, cover, remove from heat, and let sit until ready to serve.

2 Meanwhile, in a large skillet over medium-high heat, heat oil until hot but not smoking. Sauté chicken 6 minutes, or until browned.

3 In a small bowl, whisk vinegar, soy sauce, honey, garlic, and ginger. Add soy mixture to chicken, reduce heat to low, cover, and simmer 10 minutes, or until chicken is no longer pink in center. Uncover and simmer 1 to 2 minutes, or until sauce begins to thicken. Serve chicken with rice, sprinkle with scallions and sesame seeds, and serve.

BBQ Chicken Crescent Ring

No need to lasso up the family! Cowboys and cowgirls of all ages will come galloping to the dinner table as soon as they hear you're making this crescent ring for dinner. This simple, family-favorite is stuffed with a yummy-tasting barbecue chicken mixture that'll have everyone asking when you'll be making this for dinner again.

Serves 6

Ingredients

¾ cup barbecue sauce

½ cup chopped red onion

¾ cup frozen corn, thawed

2 cups shredded cooked chicken

1 cup shredded cheddar cheese

2 (8-ounce) cans refrigerated crescent rolls

Preparation

1 Preheat oven to 375 degrees F.

2 In a large skillet over medium heat, heat barbecue sauce, onion, and corn for 3 minutes; stir in chicken and cheese and heat an additional 2 minutes.

3 Unroll and separate crescent rolls into triangles. On ungreased large cookie sheet or pizza pan, arrange triangles in ring so short sides of triangles form a 5-inch circle in center. (Dough will overlap. Dough ring should look like a sun.) Spoon chicken mixture in center of each triangle. Bring smaller ends of triangles over chicken mixture, tucking ends under.

4 Bake 20 to 22 minutes, or until golden brown. Let cool 5 minutes to set-up before cutting into 12 pieces.

Note: We love using rotisserie chicken or leftover roasted chicken for this. It shreds easy and is nice and moist.

Serving Suggestion: Maybe place a bowl of sour cream, extra BBQ sauce, or hot sauce in the center of the baked ring when serving.

Easy Italian Pasta Toss

If you crave lots of flavor without having to put in a lot of time, then you'll love this pasta toss. With plenty of hearty ingredients, including penne pasta, turkey sausage, and cannellini beans, you can bet that even the most voracious eaters in your family will feel satisfied with this meal. You can go ahead and add this one to your list of family-pleasing dinners!

Serves 4

Ingredients

8 ounces penne pasta

1 tablespoon olive oil

1 pound turkey sausage, with casing removed

1 cup coarsely chopped onion

3 cloves garlic, minced

1-¾ cups chicken broth

1 (15.5-ounce) can cannellini beans, undrained

1 teaspoon dried thyme leaves

½ teaspoon salt

¼ teaspoon black pepper

5 cups packed chopped kale

¼ cup sliced sundried tomatoes in oil

Preparation

1 Cook pasta according to package directions; drain and set aside.

2 Meanwhile, in a large skillet over medium-high heat, heat oil until hot, but not smoking. Cook sausage, onion, and garlic 8 minutes, or until browned. Add broth, beans, thyme, salt, pepper, and kale and cook 5 minutes.

3 Stir in pasta and sundried tomatoes and heat 3 minutes or until everything is heated through. Serve immediately.

Turkey Bolognese with Zucchini "Spaghetti"

Transform an ordinary spaghetti dinner into an extraordinary one with this lighter weeknight version featuring a new kind of "noodle." Everyone is going to be so impressed by the taste and look of the spiralized zucchini that they won't even miss the pasta. And when it's topped with a meaty, red sauce as good as ours, you can bet it's all the better.

Serves 4

Ingredients

1 tablespoon olive oil

1 pound ground turkey

½ cup finely diced onion

½ cup finely diced carrot

2 cloves garlic, minced

½ teaspoon salt

¼ teaspoon black pepper

1 (26-ounce) jar spaghetti sauce

3 zucchini, spiralized (see note)

Grated Parmesan cheese for sprinkling

Preparation

1 In a large skillet over medium heat, heat oil until hot, but not smoking. Cook turkey, onion, carrot, garlic, salt, and pepper 8 minutes, or until no longer pink, stirring occasionally to break up turkey.

2 Add spaghetti sauce and heat 5 minutes. Add zucchini noodles, stir gently, and heat 3 to 5 minutes, or until "noodles" are tender, but not mushy. Sprinkle with Parmesan cheese and serve.

Test Kitchen Tip: *If you haven't tried spiralizing yet, now is the time! All you need is an inexpensive spiralizer, which is basically a kitchen tool that transforms some of your favorite veggies into "noodles." You can find these at most stores that sell kitchen gadgets, with prices ranging from just under $10 to fancier models that'll cost around $40 to $50.*

Thanksgiving-Stuffed Sweet Potatoes

We've come up with lots of variations on all-in-one Thanksgiving dinners, but this might just be our best idea yet. Our inspiration for this recipe came from the sweet potato casserole. While prepping it for our own Test Kitchen Thanksgiving, someone jokingly commented, "Why don't we just stuff a sweet potato with all the fixins'—sort of like a loaded baked potato?" The rest, as they say, is history (or tomorrow's tasty dinner!).

Serves 4

Ingredients

4 large sweet potatoes, washed

2 tablespoons butter, melted

2 tablespoons light brown sugar

½ teaspoon salt

¼ teaspoon black pepper

¼ cup dried cranberries

1 cup diced, cooked turkey

2 tablespoons chopped pecans

¼ cup mini marshmallows

Preparation

1 Preheat oven to 425 degrees F. Coat a baking sheet with cooking spray.

2 Pierce potatoes with a fork and place on a microwave-safe plate. Microwave 10 to 12 minutes or until tender, turning over halfway through. When cool enough to handle, cut each potato in half, lengthwise. With a soup spoon, scoop out the pulp, leaving ¼-inch thick shell. Place shells on baking sheet.

3 In a bowl, combine pulp, butter, brown sugar, salt, and pepper; mix well. Stir in cranberries and turkey. Spoon mixture into potato shells. Top evenly with nuts and marshmallows.

4 Bake for 8 to 10 minutes or until heated through and marshmallows begin to get toasty.

Super Time Saver: *Instead of cooking up a turkey breast just for this, ask the folks at the deli to cut a couple of thick slices of deli turkey. Then, simply cut it into small chunks or dice it and you are good to go!*

Lickety-Split Meat

Cupcake Meat Loaves with Mashed Potato Icing

Imagine how your family is going to look at you when you tell them you're making cupcakes for dinner. At first, they might think you've gone off your rocker, but once they see these cute cupcake meat loaves on their plates, they'll be right on board with your tasty trick. And you can bet everyone is going to love the savory potato "frosting." What a fun weeknight dinner idea!

Makes 8

Ingredients

¾ cup seasoned croutons

¼ cup water

1-½ pounds ground beef

¼ cup ketchup

1 egg, slightly beaten

1 teaspoon garlic powder

½ teaspoon salt

¼ teaspoon black pepper

2 cups refrigerated mashed potatoes, heated according to package directions

Preparation

1 Preheat oven to 375 degrees F. Coat 8 muffin tin cups with nonstick cooking spray. Place croutons in a bowl and add water, toss gently and let sit 5 minutes.

2 Meanwhile, in a large bowl, combine remaining ingredients, except mashed potatoes. Add croutons; mix well. Place ½ cup beef mixture into each of 8 muffin cups, pressing lightly.

3 Place a rimmed baking sheet under muffin tins, to catch any drippings while baking. Bake 15 to 20 minutes, or until no pink remains and juices run clear.

4 Remove "cupcakes" from the pans. (You may want to run a knife around the edges to help loosen them.)

5 Top each "cupcake" with warm mashed potatoes and serve.

Test Kitchen Tip: *After topping with the mashed potatoes, you can place these on a baking sheet and pop them under the broiler for a minute or so, until the potatoes brown up, or just sprinkle them with a little fresh parsley.*

Melt-in-Your-Mouth Steaks with Garlic-Herb Butter

Tender. Juicy. Flavorful. These are the words normally used to describe the perfect steak. But have you ever heard someone talk about a steak being so good it literally melts in their mouth? If that sounds too good to be true, just wait till you try our recipe. You'll wish you could have steak for dinner every night of the week.

Serves 2

Ingredients

½ stick plus 2 tablespoons butter, softened, divided

1 tablespoon chopped fresh garlic

1 tablespoon chopped fresh parsley

2 (12-ounce) strip steaks

¼ teaspoon kosher salt

¼ teaspoon coarsely ground black pepper

Preparation

1 In a small bowl, combine ½ stick butter, the garlic, and parsley; mix well and set aside.

2 Sprinkle steaks evenly on both sides with salt and pepper and gently press to secure onto the steak.

3 In a large skillet or grill pan over medium-high heat, melt remaining 2 tablespoons butter. Cook steaks 5 to 7 minutes per side for medium-rare, or until desired doneness.

4 Place steak on plate and top with a dollop of garlic butter. Allow to melt slightly and dig in.

Test Kitchen Tip: *This is one of the easiest, fastest, and tastiest ways to make steak. It may seem impossible that this could be made any better, but we found that if you use European-style butter, the flavor will be even richer. Look for it in your market's dairy case!*

Yee-Haw! Southwestern One Pot

Every year, people all over the country participate in their town's version of a chili cook-off. At these events, folks get together to share and show off what they believe is "the best chili ever." After attending one of our local cook-offs, we felt inspired to create a recipe that's so good it's "yee-haw"-worthy. We think you'll love this Texas-style chili so much that you might just consider entering it in next year's competition.

Serves 4

Ingredients

1 pound beef cubed steaks

2 tablespoons chili powder

2 teaspoons ground cumin

1-½ teaspoons garlic powder

¾ teaspoon dried oregano

¼ teaspoon cayenne pepper

½ teaspoon salt

2 teaspoons vegetable oil

1 onion, chopped

1 (28-ounce) can diced tomatoes, undrained

2 cups frozen corn

Preparation

1 Cut each steak lengthwise into 1-inch-wide strips, then cut crosswise into 1-inch pieces.

2 In a small bowl, mix the chili powder, cumin, garlic powder, oregano, cayenne pepper, and salt. Sprinkle beef with 2 teaspoons of seasoning mix.

3 In a large, deep skillet over high heat, heat oil until hot but not smoking. Add beef and onion and sauté until meat is browned, about 4 minutes. Add tomatoes, corn, and remaining seasoning mix. Bring to a boil, then reduce heat to medium-low and simmer, uncovered, 15 minutes, or until meat is tender.

Serving Suggestion: *This is just as good whether you serve it in a bowl or chili crock. And we think it's a good idea to top each portion with the typical chili toppings like sour cream, shredded cheese, and sliced jalapeños.*

Roast Beef Roll-Ups

It doesn't get any easier than this! Here's an idea for those nights when you don't really want to do much, but somebody's got to get dinner on the table. These roll-ups are made with basic ingredients that most of us have on-hand, but they can also be adapted to use leftovers (good thing you didn't toss yesterday's mashed potatoes!). It's recipes like this that really save the day.

Serves 3

Ingredients

2-¼ cups mashed potatoes, slightly warmed (see note)

¾ cup frozen mixed vegetables, thawed

6 slices deli roast beef (about ¾ pound total)

1 (12-ounce) jar beef gravy

½ cup water

⅓ cup French-fried onions

Preparation

1 In a medium bowl, combine mashed potatoes and vegetables; mix well. Place a ½ cup of the mixture on one end of a slice of roast beef, shaping to form a log. Roll the beef over the mixture and roll up crepe-style. Repeat with remaining roast beef slices and potato mixture.

2 In a large skillet over medium-low heat, combine gravy and water, cooking until bubbly. Add beef rolls seam-side down; cover, and simmer 10 to 15 minutes, or until heated through.

3 To serve, place 2 roll-ups on a plate, spoon gravy over top and sprinkle with French-fried onions.

Test Kitchen Tip: *You can use leftover mashed potatoes or store-bought, refrigerated, mashed potatoes, whatever is most convenient for you!*

Shortcut Italian Stuffed Peppers

Traditionally, stuffed peppers take a long time to make. First, you've got to mix the rice and the beef. Then, you've got to hollow out the peppers, stuff them, and bake them long enough so that everything is cooked just right. Well, the good news is, you can take a few shortcuts. By starting with precooked rice, cutting the peppers in half, and cooking everything in a big skillet, you save lots of time and still get the flavors you love.

Serves 6

Ingredients

1-¼ pounds ground beef

½ cup chopped onion

1 [8.8-ounce] package precooked white rice

1 teaspoon garlic powder

½ teaspoon salt

¼ teaspoon black pepper

3 green bell peppers, split lengthwise and cleaned

1 [26-ounce] jar spaghetti sauce

½ cup water

Preparation

1 In a large skillet over medium-high heat, brown beef and onion 4 to 5 minutes, stirring until meat crumbles and is no longer pink. Drain excess liquid and add rice, garlic powder, salt, and pepper; mix well. Evenly spoon mixture into pepper halves.

2 Add spaghetti sauce and water to skillet. Reduce heat to medium-low and place stuffed pepper halves in skillet. Cover and cook 15 to 20 minutes, or until heated through. Spoon sauce over peppers and serve.

Note: You can use any color pepper you like [red, green, yellow, orange]; the choice is yours!

Test Kitchen Tip: Not familiar with precooked rice? You can find it in the aisle with all the other rice varieties. It's usually in a pouch that can be quickly microwaved. If you have leftover rice or if time permits, and you want to make the rice, you'll need 2 cups.

Five Star Beef Filet with Béarnaise Sauce

Would you believe us if we told you that this steak rivals the one that you love from your favorite steakhouse? And not only that, but that you'd actually be able to do it yourself, and in less than 30 minutes? Well, you better believe it! This masterpiece is five star-worthy and ready to wow you! (Psst. This is a good one to make when the kids are out and it's just the two of you for dinner.)

Serves 2

Ingredients

2 (6-ounce) beef tenderloin filets

½ teaspoon salt

2 teaspoons coarsely ground black pepper

1 tablespoon olive oil

BÉARNAISE SAUCE
½ stick butter

2 egg yolks

2 tablespoons white wine

1 tablespoon lemon juice

½ teaspoon dried tarragon

⅛ teaspoon salt

Preparation

1 Preheat oven to 300 degrees F. Evenly sprinkle steaks with salt and pepper on both sides, gently pressing the spices onto the meat to secure.

2 In a medium skillet over medium-high heat, heat oil until hot, but not smoking; sear steaks 2 to 3 minutes per side, or until browned. Place on baking sheet.

3 Roast for about 15 minutes for medium-rare, or continue cooking to desired doneness.

4 Meanwhile, to make Béarnaise Sauce, in a small saucepan over low heat, melt butter. In a small bowl, whisk egg yolks with remaining ingredients. Slowly whisk egg mixture into the melted butter and heat 1 minute, stirring constantly, until it thickens. Serve over steaks.

Test Kitchen Tip: *When it comes to cooking thicker cuts of steaks, it's best to sear them first to seal in their juices. Then, finish cooking them at a low temperature in the oven, so that they cook evenly.*

Mom's Go-To Weeknight Goulash

Let's face it; we all grew up eating some version of this dish. Maybe you called it something different and maybe Mom used a different kind of pasta or left out the peppers, 'cause she could never get you to eat them. Either way, this is one of those weeknight staples that has stood the test of time. Moms love it for being a time-saver and kids love it because it's just so good.

Serves 4

Ingredients

½ pound elbow macaroni

1-½ pounds ground beef

½ green bell pepper, chopped

½ cup chopped onion

1 (26-ounce) jar spaghetti sauce

1 teaspoon garlic powder

½ teaspoon salt

½ teaspoon black pepper

1 cup (4 ounces) shredded Colby-Jack cheese

Preparation

1 Cook macaroni according to package directions; drain and set aside.

2 Meanwhile, in a large skillet over high heat, brown ground beef, bell pepper, and onion 6 to 8 minutes, stirring until meat crumbles and is no longer pink. Drain and return to skillet.

3 Add macaroni, spaghetti sauce, garlic powder, salt, and black pepper; mix well. Reduce heat to medium-low and cook 5 to 7 minutes, or until heated through. Sprinkle with cheese and heat 1 more minute, or until cheese is melted.

__Good for You!__ If you want to make this a little healthier for your family, just make some easy swaps. Substitute the regular pasta with whole wheat and the ground beef for ground turkey breast. (Oh, and if you're the mom who has a hard time getting the kids to eat their veggies, we suggest chopping them up really small – the veggies, not the kids!)

Chicken-Fried Steak with Milk Gravy

You haven't lived until you've had chicken-fried steak; it's practically the definition of "comfort food." Just look at it! You've got the perfectly seasoned and crunchy coating on the steak, and the simple milk gravy just smothering all of it with even more deliciousness. Really, the only thing that could make this even better is a heapin' helpin' of mashed potatoes and maybe some buttery green beans. Warning: You may need a nap after this one.

Serves 4

Ingredients

4 beef cubed steaks (1-¼ pounds total), pounded to ¼-inch thickness

1 teaspoon salt, divided

½ teaspoon black pepper, divided

¾ cup buttermilk

1 cup plus 3 tablespoons all-purpose flour

½ teaspoon paprika

½ cup vegetable oil

1-½ cups milk

Preparation

1 Sprinkle steaks evenly on both sides with ½ teaspoon salt and ¼ teaspoon pepper; set aside.

2 Place buttermilk in a shallow dish. In another shallow dish, combine 1 cup flour and the paprika. Dip steaks in buttermilk, then in flour, coating completely.

3 In a large skillet over medium-high heat, heat oil until hot, but not smoking. Add steaks and cook 3 to 4 minutes per side, or until cooked through and coating is golden. Drain on a paper towel-lined platter and cover to keep warm.

4 To the same skillet, over medium heat, add the remaining 3 tablespoons flour, the remaining ½ teaspoon salt, and the remaining ¼ teaspoon pepper to the same skillet. Cook 2 to 3 minutes, or until flour begins to turn brown, stirring constantly. Slowly stir in milk and continue to stir until it thickens, creating a gravy. Serve steaks topped with gravy.

Easy Peasy Cheesy Burger Bake

Studies show that 9 times out of 10 your family will choose burgers or pizza when given the choice for dinner... Okay, maybe there aren't any official studies that show that, but it does always seem that burgers are a top-requested dinner in most households! That's why we think you'll love this family-friendly burger bake that cooks up in no time and features all of their favorite cheesy burger flavors.

Serves 6

Ingredients

1 pound ground beef

½ cup chopped onion

½ cup ketchup

¼ cup mustard

½ teaspoon salt

¼ teaspoon black pepper

1 (13.8-ounce) can refrigerated classic pizza dough

12 (1-ounce) slices cheddar cheese, divided

1 cup hamburger dill pickle chips, drained on paper towels

Preparation

1 Preheat oven to 425 degrees F. Coat a 9- x 13-inch baking dish with cooking spray.

2 In a medium skillet over medium-high heat, brown beef and onion, stirring until meat crumbles and is no longer pink. Drain excess liquid. Add ketchup, mustard, salt, and pepper; mix well.

3 Meanwhile, unroll pizza dough and press into bottom and halfway up sides of baking dish. Top pizza dough with 6 slices cheese. Spoon the meat mixture over the cheese, then arrange pickles over that.

4 Bake 12 minutes. Top with remaining cheese slices and bake an additional 5 minutes, or until crust is browned and cheese is melted.

Fun Fact: *If you love cheeseburgers, you'll have to thank Lionel Sternberger for coming up with the combo. You see, back in 1920's, while working as a fry cook at his dad's restaurant, Sternberger decided to experiment by adding a slice of cheese to a hamburger patty. The rest, as they say, is history.*

Corn Chip Chili Dinner

You don't have to conduct a scientific study to figure out that it only takes one bite to get your family hooked on this dinner. After all, the base is made from corn chips! The way we look at it, anytime you get to have chips for dinner you're definitely winning. And when it's topped with a hearty, homemade chili, well...just go and have that bite already!

Serves 5

Ingredients

1 pound ground beef

½ cup chopped onion

½ teaspoon salt

¼ teaspoon black pepper

1 (15-ounce) can red kidney beans, undrained

1 (15-ounce) can tomato sauce

1 tablespoon chili powder

1 (9-¼-ounce) bag corn chips

½ cup fresh salsa

1 cup shredded Colby jack cheese

1 jalapeño pepper, thinly sliced (optional)

Preparation

1 In a large skillet over medium-high heat, cook beef, onion, salt, and pepper 5 to 7 minutes, stirring until meat crumbles and is no longer pink. Reduce heat to low and add beans, tomato sauce, and chili powder; simmer 15 minutes or until heated through.

2 Place corn chips on a large platter, spoon chili mixture over chips, and top evenly with salsa, cheese, and jalapeño, if desired.

Skillet Beef & Potato Wedges

Beef and potatoes are a match made in comfort food heaven. This winning combo is right up there with mac & cheese and chicken & dumplings. In this recipe, we made it even easier for you to put the two together by starting off with refrigerated potato wedges. The hardest thing about this one is deciding whether you're going to serve everyone an equal amount or give yourself a little extra.

Serves 4

Ingredients

3 tablespoons vegetable oil, divided

1 (20-ounce) package refrigerated potato wedges

1 red bell pepper, cut into ½-inch chunks

½ cup chopped onion

½ teaspoon salt

¼ teaspoon black pepper

1-¼ pounds top round steak

1 teaspoon Montreal steak seasoning

Preparation

1 In a large skillet over medium-high heat, heat 2 tablespoons oil until hot, but not smoking. Add potatoes, bell pepper, onion, salt, and pepper and sauté, covered, 10 to 12 minutes, or until potatoes begin to brown, stirring occasionally.

2 Meanwhile, evenly sprinkle steak with steak seasoning. In another skillet over medium-high heat, heat remaining 1 tablespoon oil until hot, but not smoking. Cook steak 5 minutes per side, or to desired doneness. Let steak rest 5 minutes before slicing across the grain into strips, and serve over potatoes.

Grandma's Classic Liver and Onions

In Grandma's childhood, liver and onions was a staple meal, and the way Grandma tells it...it wasn't always popular with the kids. However, somewhere along the way Grandma became a liver lover. She found that adding bacon really helped to make it even better, so she started making it that way for her kids. Now, even picky eaters will chow down on this classic dish. (We suggest holding off on letting them know what it is, until after their first bite!)

Serves 4

Ingredients

¼ pound sliced bacon

1 large onion, thinly sliced

2 tablespoons all-purpose flour

½ teaspoon salt

¼ teaspoon black pepper

4 beef liver steaks
(about 1-½ pounds total)
(see note)

Preparation

1 In a large skillet over medium heat, cook bacon 7 to 8 minutes, or until crisp. Remove bacon from skillet and set aside, leaving drippings in skillet.

2 Add onion to the bacon drippings and sauté over medium-high heat 10 minutes, or until caramelized. Remove to a bowl and cover to keep warm.

3 In a shallow dish, combine flour, salt, and pepper; mix well. Coat liver with flour mixture. Place liver in same skillet, over medium heat for 3 to 4 minutes per side, or until cooked through. (Please don't cook it until it turns to shoe leather, but just until cooked through and still juicy.) To serve, top liver with cooked onions and crumbled bacon.

Test Kitchen Tip: *If you're new to liver, we suggest swapping the beef liver with calf's liver, since it has a milder flavor to it.*

Apricot-Dijon Pork Tenderloin

Our pork tenderloin is anything but ordinary, thanks to the sweet and tangy flavor combo of apricots and Dijon mustard. Plus, since the tenderloin is a leaner cut, this is a better-for-you kind of meal. Try this the next time you're looking to cook up something different, yet delicious.

Serves 4

Ingredients

1 pound pork tenderloin

¾ teaspoon salt, divided

½ teaspoon black pepper, divided

1 tablespoon vegetable oil

1 (15-ounce) can apricot halves in syrup, drained, with syrup reserved

1 tablespoon light brown sugar

2 tablespoons apricot preserves

1 tablespoon Dijon mustard

Preparation

1 Preheat oven to 400 degrees F. Coat a baking sheet with cooking spray. Sprinkle pork evenly with ½ teaspoon salt and ¼ teaspoon pepper.

2 In a large skillet over high heat, heat oil until hot, but not smoking; sear pork 4 to 6 minutes, or until browned on all sides. Place pork on rimmed baking sheet and arrange apricots around pork. Sprinkle apricots evenly with brown sugar.

3 Roast 15 to 20 minutes, until medium or until desired doneness.

4 Meanwhile, in the same skillet over low heat, combine reserved apricot syrup, the apricot preserves, Dijon mustard, the remaining ¼ teaspoon salt, and the remaining ¼ teaspoon pepper. Heat 3 to 5 minutes, or until thickened. Slice pork, serve with apricots, and top with sauce.

Super Saucy Sicilian Pork Chops

These chops are absolutely swimming in sauce, which is just A-OK with us, since the sauce is amazing! In traditional Sicilian style, it's made with a mouthwatering blend of tomatoes, wine, onion, and spices. When poured over the pork chops, it adds a ton of flavor to every bite. (We don't even mind if some of it gets on our side dishes!)

Serves 4

Ingredients

1 (14.5-ounce) can diced tomatoes, undrained

½ cup dry white wine

1 onion, cut into half-moon slivers

1 tablespoon capers (optional)

1 teaspoon garlic powder

¼ teaspoon dried thyme leaves

½ teaspoon salt, divided

½ teaspoon black pepper, divided

2 tablespoons vegetable oil

4 (6- to 7-ounce) pork chops

Preparation

1. In a large bowl, combine tomatoes, wine, onion, capers, if desired, garlic powder, thyme, ¼ teaspoon salt, and ¼ teaspoon pepper; mix well and set aside.

2. In a large skillet over medium-high heat, heat oil until hot, but not smoking. Sprinkle pork chops evenly with remaining ¼ teaspoon salt and remaining ¼ teaspoon pepper, then brown chops about 2 minutes per side, or until golden brown.

3. Pour tomato mixture over pork chops and reduce heat to medium-low. Simmer 15 minutes, or until pork is cooked until desired doneness.

__Did You Know?__ Capers are flower buds from a shrub-like bush that grows in the Mediterranean. Before they make it to the supermarket, they're dried and pickled. Who would have ever guessed that?

Restaurant-Worthy Pork Francese

Create a restaurant dining experience for your family with this dinner that's sure to leave them speechless. Traditionally, this dish is more commonly prepared with chicken, but we found that the lemony sauce is just as great over juicy, pork medallions. They may not need to make a reservation, but they will have to help set the table!

Serves 5

Ingredients

½ cup all-purpose flour

½ teaspoon salt

¼ teaspoon black pepper

2 eggs

4 tablespoons (½ stick) butter, divided

1 pound pork tenderloin, cut into 10 slices and pounded (See note)

⅔ cup white wine

¼ cup lemon juice

1 teaspoon chopped fresh parsley

Preparation

1 In a shallow dish, combine flour, salt, and pepper; mix well. In another shallow dish, beat eggs. Coat pork in flour mixture, then dip in eggs, coating completely.

2 In a large skillet over medium heat, melt 1 tablespoon butter. Sauté pork medallions, in 2 batches, 1 to 2 minutes per side, or until golden, adding 1 tablespoon of butter to pan before second batch. Remove pork to a platter.

3 Add remaining 2 tablespoons butter, the wine, lemon juice, and parsley to skillet; mix well then return cooked pork to skillet. Cook 2 to 3 minutes, or until sauce begins to thicken and pork is cooked to desired doneness. Serve pork with sauce.

Test Kitchen Tip: *We found that the best way to flatten the pork is to place it on a cutting board, cover it with a plastic storage bag, and whack it gently with a meat mallet or a rolling pin. You want it to be about ¼-inch thick.*

"Unstuffed" Cheesy Pork Chops

Usually, stuffing is used to, well, stuff food. But, we wanted to be a little different and make things a little easier for you, so instead we put the stuffing on top of these juicy-cooked chops. And since everything is better with cheese, you know we had to add some. They're going to love every bite of this!

Serves 4

Ingredients

1 (6-ounce) package flavored stuffing mix

1 cup sliced fresh mushrooms

4 (¾-inch thick) boneless pork chops (about 1-½ pounds total)

½ teaspoon garlic powder

½ teaspoon salt

¼ teaspoon black pepper

1 tablespoon olive oil

4 (1-ounce) slices Muenster cheese

½ cup dry white wine

Preparation

1 Prepare stuffing mix according to package directions, adding mushrooms to water before water reaches boiling.

2 Meanwhile, evenly sprinkle pork chops on both sides with garlic powder, salt, and pepper. In a large skillet over medium-high heat, heat oil until hot but not smoking; cook pork chops 5 to 6 minutes, or until browned on both sides.

3 Leaving the chops in the skillet, top each pork chop with about ⅓ cup stuffing and a slice of cheese. Add wine to skillet, cover, and cook 5 minutes, or until cheese is melted and pork is cooked to desired doneness. Serve with pan juices.

Did You Know? Pork chops don't need to be cooked until well done, like it was once believed. According to the National Pork Producers Council, pork can be consumed when it's still slightly pink, has reached an internal temperature of 145 degrees F, and is allowed to rest for three minutes before serving. So, say goodbye to dry, overcooked pork, and hello to pork that's so juicy, it'll have you saying, "OOH IT'S SO GOOD!!®"

Garlic and Rosemary Lamb Chops

Add some excitement to your dinner routine by picking up something different the next time you're at the supermarket, like quick-cooking lamb chops! We like to marinate ours with lots of fresh herbs and flavorful ingredients before we finish them off in a skillet. Once your family tries these, there's no going back.

Serves 4

Ingredients

¼ cup olive oil

3 cloves garlic, thinly sliced

1 tablespoon chopped fresh rosemary

1 teaspoon lemon zest

½ teaspoon salt

¼ teaspoon black pepper

12 rib lamb chops, about 1-inch thick (about 2 pounds total)

⅓ cup white wine

1 tablespoon lemon juice

Preparation

1 In a 9- x 13-inch baking dish, combine oil, garlic, rosemary, lemon zest, salt, and pepper; mix well. Place lamb chops in marinade, coating evenly on both sides. Let sit 10 minutes.

2 In a large skillet over medium-high heat, sear lamb chops, with marinade, about 4 minutes per side. Add wine and lemon juice to skillet and continue to cook 1 to 2 minutes, or until desired doneness.

Super-Fast Seafood, Pasta, & More

Fabulous Fish Tacos

You'll never go wrong with taco night! We think our fish tacos are especially fabulous because, not only is the fish seasoned to perfection, but, they're topped with a homemade cilantro sauce that beats any other taco sauce we've ever had. Set out some cheese, sour cream, tomatoes, and jalapeño slices (for the brave ones) and let them make their own supreme versions.

Serves 4

Ingredients

¼ cup all-purpose flour

1 tablespoon chili powder

1 teaspoon ground cumin

½ teaspoon salt

1-½ pounds tilapia or other white-fleshed fish fillets, cut into 1-inch pieces

2 tablespoons vegetable oil

8 (6-inch) flour tortillas, warmed

CILANTRO SAUCE

¼ cup mayonnaise

¼ cup sour cream

2 tablespoons chopped fresh cilantro

2 teaspoons lime juice

¼ teaspoon salt

COLESLAW TOPPING

2 cups shredded coleslaw

2 tablespoons rice wine vinegar

1 tablespoon vegetable oil

Preparation

1 In a large bowl, mix flour, chili powder, cumin, and salt. Add fish and toss until evenly coated.

2 In a large skillet over medium-high heat, heat oil until hot, but not smoking. Cook fish 4 to 5 minutes or until firm, stirring occasionally.

3 Meanwhile, in a small bowl, combine Cilantro Sauce ingredients; mix well and set aside.

4 In another bowl, combine Coleslaw Topping ingredients; toss until evenly coated, and set aside.

5 Place fish evenly down the center of tortillas, then top with Coleslaw Topping and Cilantro Sauce.

Brown Sugar-Glazed Roasted Salmon

While creating this recipe we learned that some members of our Test Kitchen crew prefer not to eat salmon because it's got a "fishier" taste than some other fish. Well, our Test Kitchen Director wasn't too happy to hear that, so she came up with a recipe that would change their minds. This glazed salmon received rave reviews from everyone, including our own picky eaters; we're sure it'll do the same for yours!

Serves 4

Ingredients

2 tablespoons light brown sugar

1 tablespoon Dijon mustard

2 cloves garlic, minced

1 tablespoon chopped fresh parsley

2 tablespoons lemon juice

4 (5-ounce) salmon fillets

¼ teaspoon salt

¼ teaspoon black pepper

Preparation

1 Preheat oven to 375 degrees F. Coat a baking sheet with cooking spray.

2 In a small bowl, whisk brown sugar, mustard, garlic, parsley, and lemon juice.

3 Evenly sprinkle salmon with salt and pepper, and place on baking sheet. Spoon brown sugar and mustard glaze over salmon.

4 Roast 15 to 20 minutes, or until fish flakes easily with a fork.

Test Kitchen Tip: *When it comes to cooking fresh salmon, there's no need to cook it until it's well done. You should cook it until it flakes easily and the center is opaque. If you do prefer it to be cooked a bit longer, go ahead, just make sure it doesn't dry out.*

Potato-Crusted Catfish Fillets

For our Southern friends, local farm-raised catfish isn't anything new; actually, it's a down-home favorite. But for those of you who haven't had the chance to try it yet, just know that there's a reason why it's so popular in the South. That's because this mild-tasting white fish stays super moist when cooked and pairs well with just about anything. Here, we've gone ahead and given it a seasoned potato crust, which makes it knee-slappin' good.

Serves 4

Ingredients

1 cup instant mashed potato flakes (see Note)

½ teaspoon onion powder

½ teaspoon salt

¼ teaspoon black pepper

4 (6-ounce) U.S. farm-raised catfish fillets (about 1-½ pounds total)

6 tablespoons butter, melted

Preparation

1 Preheat oven to 375 degrees F. Coat a baking sheet with cooking spray.

2 In a shallow dish, combine potato flakes, onion powder, salt, and pepper; mix well. Dip fillets in melted butter then coat with potato mixture; place on baking sheet. Sprinkle any remaining potato mixture, evenly, over top of fillets, and press gently to secure. Drizzle with remaining butter.

3 Roast 20 to 22 minutes, or until fish flakes easily with a fork and potato crust is golden. Serve immediately.

Note: Make sure you use the dehydrated potato flakes and not the granular type instant potatoes. The consistency is very different.

Did You Know? Although we can buy catfish harvested from all over the world, we love the quality of U.S. farm-raised catfish. What makes it so good? It's raised in freshwater ponds and is fed a high-protein diet that yields a sweeter and milder flavored fish.

Macadamia-Crusted Fish with Mango Salsa

We're so excited for you to make this out-of-the-ordinary meal for your family! Buttery-rich macadamia nuts add a unique, crunchy coating to this fast-fix fish. And, to complement the saltiness, we paired it with a homemade mango salsa that's sweet and refreshing. Don't be afraid to pat yourself on the back after making this. After all, creativity should always be rewarded!

Serves 4

Ingredients

MANGO SALSA
1 ripe mango, pitted, peeled, and chopped

½ green bell pepper, finely chopped

¼ cup finely chopped red onion

2 tablespoons orange juice

¼ teaspoon salt

1 egg

2 tablespoons water

½ cup chopped macadamia nuts

⅓ cup all-purpose flour

4 (6-ounce) white-fleshed fish fillets (about 1-½ pounds total)

½ teaspoon salt

¼ teaspoon black pepper

½ stick butter

Preparation

1 In a medium bowl, combine all Mango Salsa ingredients; mix well and set aside.

2 In a shallow dish, whisk egg and water. In another shallow dish, combine nuts and flour; mix well. Evenly sprinkle fish with salt and pepper.

3 In a large skillet over medium heat, melt butter. Dip fish into egg mixture then into nut mixture, coating completely. Place fish in skillet and cook 4 to 5 minutes per side, or until golden and fish flakes easily with a fork. Top fish with Mango Salsa and serve immediately.

4-Ingredient
Spinach Dip Salmon

No, this isn't a trick. You really only need four ingredients to make the impressive looking fish on the opposite page. Does it get any easier than that? We don't think so! The spinach dip adds lots of creamy flavor, while the buttery crackers give it the crunch you crave. On those extra-busy days, don't be surprised if you find yourself coming back to this recipe.

Serves 4

Ingredients

4 (5-ounce) salmon fillets (about 1-⅓ pounds total)

½ cup prepared spinach dip

10 butter crackers, crumbled

1 tablespoon butter, melted

Preparation

1 Preheat oven to 375 degrees F. Coat a baking sheet with cooking spray. Place salmon on baking sheet. Top each fillet evenly with spinach dip.

2 In a small bowl, combine crackers and butter; mix well. Sprinkle over each fillet.

3 Roast 15 to 20 minutes, or until fish flakes easily with a fork and topping is golden.

So Many Options: *When it comes to refrigerated spinach dip, there are lots of options. We can get everything from traditional and lighter varieties to ones that have chopped artichokes and veggies in them. Maybe try a few different ones out, as each one will add its own personality to this dish.*

Gulf Coast Shrimp Boil

You can't spend a summer on the Gulf Coast without coming across a shrimp boil. They're a Southern summer tradition! Folks love this one-pot feast because it's a tasty way to bring people together, which is why it's a must-make for your family. The best part? You can enjoy a taste of summer any day of the year.

Serves 6

Ingredients

7 cups water

2 tablespoons seafood seasoning

¼ teaspoon cayenne pepper

½ teaspoon salt

1 pound smoked kielbasa, cut into 2-inch pieces

6 creamer potatoes, cut in half

1 onion, cut into quarters

3 ears corn, cut into 3-inch pieces

1 pound large shrimp, unpeeled

Preparation

1 In a soup pot, combine the water, seafood seasoning, cayenne pepper, and salt. Cover and bring to a boil over high heat. Add kielbasa, potatoes, onion, and corn; re-cover, and cook 15 minutes, or until potatoes are fork-tender.

2 Add shrimp and cook 2 minutes, or until shrimp are pink and cooked through.

3 Drain liquid, reserving 2 cups for dunking. Serve immediately.

Serving Suggestion: *Make sure you have a couple of loaves of crusty bread for dunking, so you don't miss out on any of the flavorful liquid! And if you want to recreate an authentic Gulf Coast-style shrimp boil, serve on newspaper instead of plates (this makes for easy cleanup too!).*

Chesapeake-Style Crab Cakes

No trip to Maryland would be complete without a taste of their crab cakes, but it isn't so easy to schlep the whole family to the bay when those cravings come calling. That's why we've made it easy for you to provide a Chesapeake dining experience for your family whenever and wherever you want. Ya might say these no-fuss crab cakes are perfect no matter where or when you serve them!

Makes 6

Ingredients

1 egg

2 tablespoons finely chopped celery

2 tablespoons finely sliced scallion

1 tablespoon Worcestershire sauce

1 teaspoon yellow mustard

¼ teaspoon salt

¼ teaspoon black pepper

¾ cup plain bread crumbs

2 (8-ounce) containers refrigerated lump crabmeat, drained well

1 tablespoon vegetable oil

Preparation

1 In a medium bowl, combine egg, celery, scallion, Worcestershire sauce, mustard, salt, and pepper; mix well. Stir in bread crumbs and crabmeat; mix gently until well combined. Form mixture into 6 patties.

2 In a large skillet over medium heat, heat oil until hot, but not smoking; cook crab cakes 4 to 5 minutes per side, or until golden brown and heated through.

Decisions, Decisions: *If you want to make these cocktail-sized, go ahead. These can be made as small as you like, so you can have them for dinner, serve them as an appetizer, or even as a snack.*

Garlic-Lime Shrimp Rice Bowl

Lose the tortilla and serve up some true Tex-Mex flavors in colorful bowls! From the bright yellow corn and ripe red tomato to the green avocado and plump pink shrimp, these rice bowls are pretty as can be and full of fresh tastes. Plus, the winning combo of garlic, lime, and cilantro helps bring all the flavors together, to make these even more irresistible.

Serves 4

Ingredients

1-½ cups instant white rice

6 tablespoons butter

2 tablespoons olive oil

1 pound large shrimp, peeled and deveined

4 cloves garlic, minced

2 tablespoon chopped fresh cilantro

½ teaspoon salt

¼ teaspoon black pepper

1 large tomato, diced

1 cup frozen corn, thawed

¼ cup chopped red onion

1 avocado, peeled, pitted, and sliced

1 fresh lime, squeezed

Preparation

1 Cook rice according to package directions; keep covered to keep warm.

2 Meanwhile, in a large skillet over medium heat, melt butter with oil. Sauté shrimp and garlic 3 to 5 minutes, or until shrimp are pink. Stir in cilantro, salt, and pepper.

3 Evenly divide rice into bowls. Top with equal amounts of tomato, corn, onion, and avocado slices, as shown. Spoon shrimp mixture evenly on top, drizzle with lime juice, and serve.

Test Kitchen Tip: *When it comes time to buy your shrimp, look for ones that are marked large or extra-large, with a count per pound of 20 to 30.*

Faster-Than-Takeout Shrimp Fried Rice

Chinese food cravings can be serious. When you get them, it's best to satisfy them fast; otherwise, you might find yourself ordering one of everything on the menu. Luckily, this takeout-style fried rice cooks up quicker than it takes for you to place an order and wait for the delivery guy to bring it. Plus, since it's homemade you can tweak it to fit your family's preferences.

Serves 6

Ingredients

2 cups water

2 cups instant white rice

1 egg

2 tablespoons vegetable oil

1 pound large raw shrimp, peeled and deveined

½ teaspoon garlic powder

1 cup frozen peas and carrots, thawed

¼ cup soy sauce

Preparation

1 In a medium saucepan over high heat, bring water to a boil. Stir in rice, cover, and remove from heat; set aside 8 minutes, then fluff with a fork.

2 Meanwhile, over medium-high heat, in a large skillet coated with cooking spray, scramble egg into small pieces. When egg is set, remove from skillet and set aside.

3 Heat oil in skillet. Evenly sprinkle shrimp with garlic powder and sauté 2 minutes. Add peas and carrots to skillet and heat 2 more minutes. Add rice and soy sauce and cook 3 to 5 minutes, or until heated through, stirring occasionally. Stir in scrambled egg and serve.

A Little Lighter: *If you're watching your sodium, go ahead and swap out the regular soy sauce with the low-sodium kind. By doing so, you'll reduce the sodium from the soy sauce by about 35 percent. Now that's good news!*

Something New Shrimp Pizza

Don't let pizza night get boring! Sure, your pepperoni and cheese pie may be great, but, every once in a while, it's nice to try something new. For this one, we were inspired by the flavors of summer, so we swapped out the red sauce for something lighter and piled on some of our favorite summer veggies. Once we realized that shrimp would make the perfect protein for this pizza, we knew that we had come up with a real winner.

Serves 4

Ingredients

1 (13.8-ounce) package refrigerated pizza crust

½ cup fresh cilantro

⅓ cup olive oil

2 cloves garlic

½ teaspoon salt

8 ounces frozen cooked shrimp, thawed, with tails removed

1 cup frozen corn, thawed

¼ cup chopped red bell pepper

2 tablespoons chopped red onion

1 cup shredded mozzarella cheese

Preparation

1 Preheat oven to 400 degrees F. Coat a 10- x 15-inch rimmed baking sheet with cooking spray. Unroll pizza crust and press into baking sheet. Bake 5 minutes or until par-baked.

2 Meanwhile, in a blender or food processor, combine cilantro, oil, garlic, and salt; blend until smooth. Brush 2 tablespoons of cilantro mixture onto the crust and set aside.

3 Pour remaining cilantro mixture into a medium bowl. Add shrimp, corn, bell pepper, and onion; mix well. Evenly spoon the shrimp mixture over crust and sprinkle with cheese.

4 Bake 8 to 10 minutes, or until cheese is melted and crust is golden. Cut into 8 slices and serve.

Seared Scallops with Sun Dried Tomato Aioli

You've seen dishes like this in restaurants and, maybe, at special catered events, but now, it's time to bring home the fancy! Perfectly seared scallops are teamed with a homemade aioli (that's just a fancy name for an olive oil-based sauce) for a flavor explosion that's unlike any other. Served over some wilted spinach, this dish is going to earn you some serious bragging rights. They may even wonder if you've got plans to open up a restaurant of your own...

Serves 4

Ingredients

SUN DRIED TOMATO AIOLI
2 tablespoons olive oil

¼ cup sun dried tomatoes in oil, plus 2 tablespoons oil from tomatoes

1 clove garlic

⅛ teaspoon salt

⅛ teaspoon black pepper

1 pound sea scallops

½ teaspoon salt

¼ teaspoon black pepper

2 tablespoons olive oil, divided

1 (10-ounce) package fresh spinach

Preparation

1 In a blender or food processor, combine olive oil, sun dried tomatoes, oil from tomatoes, garlic, salt, and pepper. Blend 10 to 15 seconds, or until pureed. Set aside.

2 Place scallops on a plate lined with paper towels, and pat dry with another paper towel. Season with salt and pepper.

3 In a large skillet over medium-high heat, heat 1 tablespoon olive oil. Place scallops in skillet and cook 2 to 3 minutes per side, until each side is golden and the center is firm.

4 Remove scallops to a plate; cover with foil to keep warm. In the same skillet, heat remaining 1 tablespoon olive oil; sauté spinach 2 minutes, or until wilted, stirring frequently. Serve scallops over spinach and top with Sun Dried Tomato Aioli.

Did You Know? *Sea scallops are the big ones, and bay scallops are the little ones. It's easy to remember if you just keep in mind that the sea is always bigger than the bay.*

Simple Skillet "Baked" Ziti

You'll make this one again and again, and then again! It's not just that it's so simple or that it's so quick; it's more about the fact that it tastes like something you just want to dive into head first. No, really, between the hearty sausage, the fill-ya-up pasta, and the saucy-cheesiness, it's like a pasta lover's dream come true. It's sure to put some smiles on their faces when you add this to your week's dinner menu.

Serves 4

Ingredients

8 ounces penne pasta

1 tablespoon olive oil

1-¼ pounds Italian sausage, cut into thirds

1 green bell pepper, cut into 1-inch chunks

½ cup chopped onion

1 (24-ounce) jar spaghetti sauce

1 cup shredded mozzarella cheese

Preparation

1 Prepare pasta according to package directions; drain and set aside.

2 Meanwhile, in a large skillet over medium-high heat, heat oil until hot, but not smoking. Sauté sausage 7-8 minutes or until browned, turning occasionally. Add bell pepper and onion and continue cooking 7 to 8 minutes, or until sausage is no longer pink in center.

3 Add sauce and cooked pasta; tossing gently to combine. Heat about 3 minutes, then sprinkle with cheese, cover, and cook 3 to 5 minutes, or until cheese is melted.

Whirly-Twirly
Mac 'n' Cheese

Put down the blue box and let us show you what really great macaroni and cheese is supposed to taste like. You see, we're firm believers that the best mac 'n' cheese is made with more than one kind of cheese, so we've combined two different ones in this recipe. What you get is a perfectly creamy and flavorful mac 'n' cheese (made with spaghetti!) that you'll want to keep whirling-and-twirling onto your fork and into your mouth.

Serves 6

Ingredients

1 pound spaghetti

½ stick butter

¼ cup all-purpose flour

3 cups milk

3 cups shredded sharp cheddar cheese

8 ounces Gouda cheese, shredded

1 teaspoon dry mustard

1 teaspoon salt

½ teaspoon black pepper

Preparation

1 In a soup pot, cook spaghetti according to package directions; drain and set aside.

2 Meanwhile, in a medium saucepan over medium heat, melt butter, then stir in flour. Gradually stir in milk and cook 3 to 5 minutes, or until thickened, stirring frequently. Add cheeses, dry mustard, salt, and pepper, and stir 3 to 5 minutes, or until cheese is melted.

3 Return spaghetti to soup pot, add cheese sauce, and mix until evenly coated. Cook on low heat 2 to 3 minutes, or until heated through, stirring constantly. Serve immediately.

Change It Up: *For more color and nutrition, you can stir in a cup of thawed, frozen peas when you add the pasta to the cheese sauce.*

Speedy Spaghetti and Homemade Meatballs

Spaghetti and meatballs is the classic Italian comfort food; it's easy to make and everyone loves it. And to make ours extra-special we decided to make the meatballs from scratch, using a blend of beef and pork. We think this combo is what makes the meatballs really tender and packed with flavor. You might even find these taste better than the ones Grandma makes, and if they do...don't tell her (or anybody).

Serves 6

Ingredients

1 pound spaghetti

¾ pound ground beef

¾ pound ground pork

¾ cup plain bread crumbs

½ cup grated Parmesan cheese

1 cup water, divided

2 tablespoons chopped fresh parsley

1 egg

1-½ teaspoons garlic powder

1 teaspoon salt

¾ teaspoon black pepper

1 (24-ounce) jar spaghetti sauce

Preparation

1 Cook spaghetti according to package directions. Drain and set aside.

2 Meanwhile, in a large bowl, combine beef, pork, bread crumbs, Parmesan cheese, ½ cup water, the parsley, egg, garlic powder, salt, and pepper; gently mix until well combined. Form mixture into 12 equal-sized meatballs.

3 Coat a large skillet with cooking spray. Cook meatballs over medium-high heat about 8 minutes, or until browned, turning them occasionally. Add spaghetti sauce and remaining ½ cup water. Cover and cook 8 to 10 minutes, or until meatballs are no longer pink in center.

4 Serve the spaghetti topped with the sauce and the meatballs on the side. (This way they won't roll off the plate when you try to cut into them.)

Mediterranean Ravioli with Feta Crumbles

Most of us don't have time to make ravioli from scratch on the weekend, never mind on a busy weeknight. But that doesn't mean we should give up on one of our favorite pasta dishes! Thanks to shortcuts like frozen ravioli, we can create mouthwatering meals like this in a cinch. In this version, we add a homemade fresh tomato sauce, a couple of veggies, and feta cheese for a classic Mediterranean twist.

Serves 4

Ingredients

1 (24-ounce) package frozen cheese ravioli

¼ cup olive oil

3 tomatoes, chopped

½ cup chopped onion

3 cloves garlic, minced

½ teaspoon dried oregano

½ teaspoon salt

¼ teaspoon black pepper

2 cups fresh spinach

¼ cup sliced black olives

¼ cup crumbled feta cheese

Preparation

1 Cook ravioli according to package directions; drain well and set aside.

2 Meanwhile, in a large skillet over medium-high heat, heat oil until hot, but not smoking. Cook tomatoes, onion, garlic, oregano, salt, and pepper for 8 minutes, or until the tomatoes start to break down.

3 Add ravioli, spinach, and olives and heat 5 minutes, or until heated through. Sprinkle with feta cheese and serve.

Finishing Touch: *Feel free to garnish each serving with some fresh chopped tomatoes and a sprig of fresh oregano.*

Better-than-Ever Lasagna Planks

Lasagna has always been good, but now it's better-than-ever, because we've found a way to make it in under 30 minutes without sacrificing any of the good stuff. Instead of cooking it in a traditional casserole form, we layer our ingredients on individual noodles ("planks"). So, you still get the beefy, the cheesy, and the saucy, but you don't have to spend lots of time prepping and baking.

Serves 4

Ingredients

4 lasagna noodles

½ pound ground beef

1 cup spaghetti sauce

1 (15-ounce) container ricotta cheese

1-½ cups shredded mozzarella cheese, divided

1 teaspoon garlic powder

½ teaspoon salt

Preparation

1 In a large pot of boiling water, cook lasagna noodles 8 to 9 minutes, or until tender; drain and lay flat.

2 Meanwhile, in a medium skillet over medium-high heat, cook ground beef 4 to 5 minutes, or until browned; drain off excess liquid. Stir in spaghetti sauce and heat 2 minutes.

3 In a medium bowl, combine ricotta cheese, 1 cup mozzarella cheese, the garlic powder, and salt; mix well.

4 Cut lasagna noodles in half (they're easier to serve this way) and place on a baking sheet. Spread ricotta mixture evenly over noodles. Spoon ground beef over ricotta mixture, then sprinkle with remaining ½ cup mozzarella cheese.

5 Preheat broiler to high. Broil lasagna 2 minutes, or until cheese is melted.

Potato Gnocchi with Vodka Sauce

Here's a dish that's weeknight-simple, as well as jaw-dropping good and fits any occasion. Just imagine, heavenly potato nuggets covered in the richest vodka sauce you've ever tasted. We actually think that the sauce is so darn good, you might have a hard time resisting eating it by the spoonful as it simmers on your stove. And as tempting as that may sound, we promise it's better when served over the gnocchi!

Serves 4

Ingredients

1 (17.5-ounce) package gnocchi

2 tablespoons olive oil

2 tablespoons butter

¼ cup finely chopped onion

1 cup canned crushed tomatoes

½ cup heavy cream

¾ teaspoon salt

¾ teaspoon black pepper

⅓ cup vodka

1 tablespoon slivered fresh basil

Preparation

1 Prepare gnocchi according to package directions; drain and set aside.

2 Meanwhile, in a large skillet over medium heat, heat oil and butter until butter is melted. Add onion and sauté about 3 minutes, or until tender, but not browned. Add tomatoes, heavy cream, salt, and pepper. Cook 3 minutes, stirring occasionally. Add vodka and continue cooking 2 minutes, or until sauce thickens, stirring occasionally.

3 Add gnocchi to sauce and mix until incorporated. Serve topped with slivers of fresh basil.

Did You Know? *Gnocchi are mini dumplings that are made from potatoes and typically served with sauce. They're cooked similar to pasta and are very hearty, so a little go a long way.*

All-In-One
Beef 'n' Noodles

This dinner is lip-smackin' and noodle-slurpin' good (no, really, it's hard to resist doing either of those things when you eat this yummy dish). Since kids of all ages (that's you too!) love spaghetti-shaped pasta, we created this beefed-up version where everything cooks in one pan; yes, even the pasta. Now, go ahead and chow down with gusto!

Serves 4

Ingredients

12 ounces spaghetti, uncooked, broken in half

1 (28-ounce) can diced tomatoes, undrained

1 onion, thinly sliced

3 cloves garlic, minced

4 cups beef broth

2 teaspoons Italian seasoning

½ teaspoon salt

2 tablespoons olive oil

1 pound ground beef

½ teaspoon black pepper

Grated Parmesan cheese for topping

Preparation

1 In a soup pot, combine spaghetti, tomatoes with liquid, onion, and garlic. Pour in beef broth and sprinkle with Italian seasoning and salt. Drizzle oil over top and cover.

2 Bring to a boil over medium-high heat, then reduce heat to medium-low, uncover, and cook 10 minutes, or until liquid has reduced by half, stirring every 2 to 3 minutes.

3 Meanwhile, in a medium skillet over high heat, cook ground beef and pepper 5 to 6 minutes, or until no longer pink; drain. Add beef to pasta mixture, mix well, and serve with Parmesan cheese on top.

Italian Hoagie Stromboli

A stromboli is sort of like a rolled up pizza, and just like you would with a pizza, you can pretty much put whatever you want in it. In this case, we went with some of our favorite Italian hoagie toppings. Now, we know that most strombolis have the sauce on the inside, but we thought it'd be fun for your family to dunk as they please. So, set out some crocks with warm marinara sauce and get dunkin'!

Serves 4

Ingredients

1 (13.8-ounce) package refrigerated pizza crust

6 slices deli-style ham

12 thin slices deli-style pepperoni

12 slices provolone cheese

1 cup roasted red pepper strips

1 teaspoon Italian seasoning

½ teaspoon garlic powder

Cooking spray

1 tablespoon grated Parmesan cheese

Preparation

1 Preheat oven to 425 degrees F. Coat a baking sheet with cooking spray.

2 Unroll pizza crust dough onto a clean counter. Layer evenly with ham, pepperoni, provolone cheese, and roasted peppers. Sprinkle with Italian seasoning and garlic powder.

3 Starting at one end of the dough, roll up jellyroll-style and place on baking sheet seam side-down. Lightly spray dough with cooking spray then sprinkle with Parmesan cheese.

4 Bake 15 to 18 minutes, or until golden. Cut into 8 slices and serve.

In-a-Jiff
Go-Alongs

Grandma Elsie's Broccoli Casserole

Regular viewers of our TV segments will know that we've had quite a few grandmas visit our Test Kitchen and share their best recipes with us. While not all grandmas love to be on TV, many of them are willing to cook up some fun and swap stories about their most-requested recipes. This one comes from a spirited grandma named Elsie, who says her grandchildren always devour her creamy broccoli casserole. Her best tip? "Add lots of T.L.C.!"

Serves 8

Ingredients

4 cups broccoli florets

¼ cup chicken broth

1 (10-½-ounce) can condensed cream of mushroom soup, undiluted

½ cup (2 ounces) shredded sharp cheddar cheese

¼ cup mayonnaise

1-½ teaspoons lemon juice

1 teaspoon garlic powder

½ teaspoon black pepper

¼ cup crispy fried onions, crushed

Preparation

1 Coat a 2-quart baking dish with cooking spray. Add broccoli and broth, cover tightly with plastic wrap, and microwave on high 7 minutes.

2 In a medium bowl, combine remaining ingredients except crispy fried onions; stir well, then spoon over cooked broccoli mixture.

3 Cover with plastic wrap and microwave on high 4 to 5 minutes, or until sauce is heated and broccoli is tender. Top with crispy fried onions and serve immediately.

__Did You Know?__ The wattage in microwaves varies a great deal, which affects cooking time. As a general rule, the higher the wattage, the faster things cook. Just keep that in mind whenever you're following a recipe that involves microwave cooking.

Buttery Pecan Green Beans

Forget the days of trying to bribe your kids to eat their green veggies. When they taste how buttery and delicious these green beans are, they're going to gobble them up faster than you can imagine. As an added bonus, there's a nice crunch from the toasted pecans, too! Isn't it great when you find easy solutions to some of your biggest dinnertime concerns?

Serves 5

Ingredients

1 pound fresh green beans, trimmed

½ cup pecan halves

½ stick butter

¼ teaspoon salt

⅛ teaspoon black pepper

Preparation

1 In a medium saucepan over high heat, place beans in enough water to cover. Bring to a boil and cook 6 to 8 minutes, or until tender; drain well.

2 Meanwhile, in a skillet, over medium heat, sauté pecans in butter until butter is lightly browned and pecans are toasted.

3 Add green beans to skillet, sprinkle with salt and pepper, tossing until evenly coated, and serve.

Good For You! *A ½ cup of pecans has more than 4 grams of protein and 5 grams of good-for-you fiber. Now that's something to go nuts over!*

Muffin Tin Carrot Bake

You might think that we put these into the wrong chapter, but we promise you it was totally intentional. You see, these aren't ordinary muffins. They're made with carrots, which makes them a great go-along with your savory main dishes. This unique idea for serving up a favorite veggie is going to leave everyone speechless. Just wait till they discover what the main ingredient for getting them so moist and "carrot-y" is!

Makes 12

Ingredients

3 (4-ounce) jars carrot baby food

1 stick butter, melted

3 eggs

1 cup all-purpose flour

1 cup packed light brown sugar

1 tablespoon lemon juice

1 teaspoon vanilla extract

1 teaspoon baking soda

1 teaspoon baking powder

½ teaspoon salt

Preparation

1 Preheat oven to 350 degrees F. Coat a 12-cup muffin tin with cooking spray.

2 In a large bowl, combine baby food and butter; mix well. Add remaining ingredients; mix until everything is well blended. Pour evenly into muffin cups.

3 Bake 15 to 17 minutes, or until a toothpick comes out clean.

Did You Know? *We use baby food because it's an easy way to get perfectly pureed carrots that make these muffins super smooth and very satisfying.*

Blistered Tomatoes Italiano

These bite-sized tomatoes are so much fun to pop into your mouth! While we love cherry tomatoes as-is, we wanted to share a new way for your family to enjoy them with dinner. They can be served on the side or on top of a nice piece of grilled meat. We especially love them in the summer, when tomatoes are at their peak.

Serves 4

Ingredients

2 teaspoons olive oil

1 (12-ounce) container cherry tomatoes

¼ cup Italian dressing

1 tablespoon slivered basil

Preparation

1 In a large skillet over high heat, heat oil until hot, but not smoking; add tomatoes and sauté 5 to 6 minutes, or until tomatoes begin to blister and brown, stirring occasionally.

2 Remove from heat, add Italian dressing and basil, and toss until evenly coated.

So Many Options: *Although the recipe calls for cherry tomatoes, it's no problem if you want to use grape tomatoes. They're very similar, except the grape tomatoes are more oval in shape, a bit smaller, and a little less sweet than the cherry tomatoes.*

Happy Harvest Brussels Sprouts

There are so many great fruits and veggies that are harvested in the fall. There's apples and pumpkins, squashes and sweet potatoes, Brussels sprouts and cranberries...and so much more. If you love fall flavors as much as we do, then you're going to be all about this go-along that offers some of our favorite tastes of the harvest. It's up to you to decide whether you want to wait until the leaves start changing colors to make this one!

Serves 7

Ingredients

2 tablespoons olive oil, divided

½ cup chopped onion

½ cup coarsely chopped walnuts

½ cup dried cranberries

1 pound Brussels sprouts, cut in half and thinly sliced

¾ teaspoon salt

¼ teaspoon black pepper

Preparation

1 In a large skillet over medium heat, heat 1 tablespoon oil until hot, but not smoking; cook onions 3 to 4 minutes, or until tender. Add walnuts and cranberries and cook 3 minutes, or until nuts are lightly toasted.

2 Add remaining 1 tablespoon oil, the Brussels sprouts, salt, and pepper and cook 5 minutes, or until shredded sprouts just start to wilt, stirring occasionally.

Good for You: *If you're not eating cabbage or Brussels sprouts as part of your regular diet, then you're missing out! Besides tasting great, these veggies are loaded with potassium, fiber, vitamin C, and other important nutrients.*

Fiesta Skillet Corn

You'll be doing the cha-cha all the way to the dining room table when you make this colorful corn go-along. Bursting with flavor from all the great add-ins, this corn is a perfect choice for your weeknight summer menu. Pair it with your favorite burgers, pulled pork, or shredded chicken for a meal that's sure to have everyone smiling from ear to ear (pun intended!).

Serves 4

Ingredients

4 slices bacon

1 (12-ounce) package frozen corn, thawed

½ red bell pepper, chopped

½ teaspoon salt

¼ teaspoon black pepper

1 tablespoon butter

3 scallions, sliced

Preparation

1 In a large skillet over medium heat, cook bacon 5 to 7 minutes, or until crispy. Reserving drippings in skillet, remove bacon to a paper towel-lined plate, then crumble.

2 In the same skillet, in the bacon drippings, combine corn, bell pepper, salt, and pepper; sauté 5 minutes. Add butter, scallions, and half the bacon; heat 2 minutes. Top with remaining bacon and serve.

Test Kitchen Tip: *To thaw corn quickly, you can either microwave it for about 1-½ minutes or place it in a strainer and run warm water over it.*

Garden Fresh Italian Zucchini

In the summer, when your garden is overflowing with zucchini and tomatoes, you've got to make this fresh-tasting go-along. And if you don't have a garden, you can just visit your local farmer's market. All we're saying is, you don't want to miss out on this summertime staple. Pair it with your favorite grilled foods (maybe a nice piece of chicken or fish) or maybe serve it with some pasta. Either way, you're going to find it delicious!

Serves 5

Ingredients

2 tablespoons olive oil

2 zucchini, cut into 1-inch chunks

1 onion, cut into ½-inch chunks

5 plum tomatoes, cut into 1-inch chunks

3 cloves garlic, minced

½ teaspoon Italian seasoning

½ teaspoon salt

¼ teaspoon black pepper

Preparation

1 In a large skillet over medium heat, heat oil until hot, but not smoking. Add zucchini and onion and cook 10 minutes, stirring occasionally.

2 Add remaining ingredients and cook 5 minutes, or until zucchini is tender, stirring occasionally.

Penny Pincher's Ramen Noodles

There's nothing wrong with wanting to save money, especially when it comes to getting dinner on the table. One of our favorite ways to "pinch pennies" is to use ramen noodles. These noodles are budget-friendly and, with a little creativity, can be transformed into mouthwatering dishes (like the one you see on the opposite page). Not only is this a win for your palate, but it's a win for your wallet, too.

Serves 6

Ingredients

2 tablespoons sesame oil

2 (3-ounce) packages ramen noodles, reserving seasoning packets for another use (see note)

1-½ cups chicken broth

8 ounces fresh sugar snap peas

1 (8-ounce) can water chestnuts, drained

¼ cup chopped red bell pepper

Preparation

1 In a large skillet over medium heat, heat oil until hot, but not smoking. Break up noodles and add to skillet; cooking 4 to 5 minutes, or until browned, stirring constantly.

2 Add broth, sugar snap peas, water chestnuts, and red pepper. Cook 6 to 8 minutes, or until all liquid is absorbed and noodles are tender, stirring occasionally. Serve immediately.

Did You Know? *It doesn't really matter which flavor variety of ramen noodles you pick up, since the only difference between them is the seasoning packet. Because we're not using it in this recipe, feel free to use whatever you have on hand.*

Perfect Pepperoni Mac & Cheese

There's about a million and one different ways to make macaroni and cheese, and everyone has their favorite. Luckily, there's not really a wrong way to go, since it's all about what you like best! In this recipe, we added pepperoni to our macaroni and cheese, so that the spices from the pepperoni seep into the sauce, making it super flavorful. For some, this is the best macaroni and cheese ever and it goes perfectly with everything.

Serves 6

Ingredients

2 cups elbow macaroni

3 tablespoons butter

2 tablespoons all-purpose flour

2 cups milk

3 cups shredded cheddar cheese

1 teaspoon salt

¼ teaspoon black pepper

⅓ cup pepperoni slices, cut in half

Preparation

1 Cook macaroni according to package directions; drain and set aside.

2 Meanwhile, in a large skillet over medium heat, melt butter. Whisk in flour until smooth, and cook 1 minute. Slowly whisk in milk, bring to a boil, and cook until thickened, stirring constantly. Add cheese, salt, and pepper, and continue cooking until cheese is melted, stirring constantly.

3 Add macaroni to skillet. Stir in pepperoni and cook 3 to 5 minutes, or until heated through.

Crave-Worthy Cabbage & Pasta

Do you ever feel like you have to "sell" your family on eating certain kinds of veggies? You find yourself saying things like, "But you'll love it THIS way" or "It's so good for your body!" Well, we can almost guarantee that this is a no-selling-required recipe. They'll be hooked in by the buttery bowties, but they'll stay for all the other flavors they'll taste. You're going to feel so proud!

Serves 6

Ingredients

8 ounces bowtie pasta

6 tablespoons butter

1 cup coarsely chopped onion

4 cups thickly shredded cabbage (about ½ of a medium head)

1-½ cups sliced fresh mushrooms

1 teaspoon garlic powder

1 teaspoon salt

¼ teaspoon black pepper

Preparation

1 Cook bowtie pasta according to package directions; drain and set aside.

2 Meanwhile, in a large skillet over high heat, melt butter; sauté onion and cabbage 8 to 10 minutes, or until they begin to brown. Add mushrooms, garlic powder, salt, and pepper, and continue to cook 5 minutes.

3 Add pasta and heat 5 minutes, or until mixture is heated through. Serve immediately.

Fancy-Schmancy Mushroom Quinoa

This side dish does double duty. It allows you to show off your fancy-schmancy side and it gets your family to try something new. They might be a little hesitant at first, but you stay your course and let them know that they're going to love how creamy and savory this one is. Don't worry, once everyone's taken a bite, you won't have any more convincing to do. This risotto-like side is going to prove itself a winner.

Serves 6

Ingredients

2 teaspoons olive oil

2 tablespoons finely diced onion

2 cloves garlic, minced

1 cup quinoa

2 cups chicken broth

1 cup sliced fresh mushrooms

¼ teaspoon salt

½ cup crumbled goat cheese

1 tablespoon diced roasted red pepper

1 tablespoon slivered fresh basil

Preparation

1 In a medium saucepan over medium heat, heat oil until hot, but not smoking. Add onion and garlic and cook 2 to 3 minutes, or until tender. Add quinoa, chicken broth, mushrooms, and salt. Bring to a boil over high heat.

2 Reduce heat to low, cover, and cook 15 to 20 minutes, or until liquid is absorbed.

3 Stir in goat cheese, roasted red pepper, and basil just until lightly mixed. Serve immediately.

Salt & Vinegar Roasted Potatoes

Do you love salt and vinegar potato chips so much you find yourself eating them right out of the bag by the handful? If you do, then you'll love our roasted potatoes seasoned with a drizzle of malt vinegar and sprinkled with a bit of salt. They're absolutely addictive!

Serves 6

Ingredients

1-½ pounds small creamer potatoes, cut in half

2 tablespoons olive oil

½ teaspoon salt

¼ teaspoon black pepper

Malt vinegar for drizzling

Preparation

1 Preheat oven to 450 degrees F.

2 In a medium bowl, combine potatoes, oil, salt, and pepper; toss until evenly coated. Place potatoes on a baking sheet.

2 Roast 20 minutes, or until potatoes are fork tender and they begin to brown. Place potatoes in a bowl and drizzle with malt vinegar. Serve immediately.

So Many Options: *If you like your 'tater's on the saltier side, then sprinkle on some sea salt or kosher salt right after drizzling them with the vinegar.*

Super-Fast Loaded Potato Casserole

This side dish has everything going for it; it's almost too good to be true! First off, it's made with only five ingredients. Secondly, it's like the creamiest, cheesiest, yummiest potato casserole ever. And finally, it's super fast...you could make it in under 15 minutes from the moment you've gathered your ingredients to the time it's ready to serve. Honestly, why would you even think of another potato casserole after this one?

Serves 6

Ingredients

1 (24-ounce) package refrigerated mashed potatoes

2 tablespoons ready-to-serve bacon pieces

1 tablespoon sour cream

3 scallions, sliced

½ cup shredded cheddar cheese

Preparation

1 In a 1-quart microwave-safe dish, combine potatoes, bacon, sour cream, and scallions; mix well.

2 Microwave on high 5 to 6 minutes, or until hot in center.

3 Meanwhile, heat broiler to high. Sprinkle cheese over potatoes and broil 2 to 3 minutes, or until the top is golden.

Test Kitchen Tip: *If you prefer to make your mashed potatoes from scratch, go for it. It will add another 20 minutes or so to the recipe, but that's up to you.*

Out-of-the-Ordinary Potato Salad

Your family probably has a few favorite potato salads that you make on occasion, but what if you added a new one to the mix just to change things up? In this tasty version, we wanted fresher flavors, so we left out the mayo and went with a citrusy vinaigrette. It's the perfect complement to the mix of potatoes and other fresh veggies in this inspiring go-along, and your family is going to eat it right up.

Serves 6

Ingredients

1 (20-ounce) package refrigerated diced potatoes

¼ cup water

¼ cup olive oil

2 tablespoons red wine vinegar

1 tablespoon lemon juice

3 cloves garlic, minced

1 teaspoon salt

¼ teaspoon black pepper

2 cups spinach, coarsely chopped

½ cup cherry tomatoes, cut in half

¼ cup chopped red onion

¼ cup Kalamata olives, drained

Preparation

1 In a large microwave-safe bowl, combine potatoes and water; cover with plastic wrap. Microwave 5 to 7 minutes, or until fork-tender; drain off excess water.

2 Meanwhile, in a small bowl, whisk oil, vinegar, lemon juice, garlic, salt, and pepper.

3 Add remaining ingredients to potatoes, drizzle with oil mixture, and gently toss until evenly coated. Serve immediately, or refrigerate until ready to serve.

Garlic & Herb Pierogies

All right, all right, we know that Babcia (that's Polish for "grandma") used to make her pierogies from scratch in the Old Country, but, back then, there was a whole lot more time to do things like that. Nowadays, we've learned to improvise a little! In this recipe, we've added some homemade touches to shortcut frozen pierogies. Serve these to your family (including Babcia!), so everyone can appreciate how "old" can become "new" again!

Serves 5

Ingredients

1 cup chicken broth

1 (6.5-ounce) container garlic and herb cheese spread

¼ teaspoon black pepper

1 (16-ounce) package frozen potato and cheese pierogies

2 scallions, sliced

Preparation

1 In a large skillet over medium heat, combine broth, cheese spread, and pepper; whisk until cheese is melted. Add pierogies, cover, and cook 10 minutes, or until heated through.

2 Sprinkle with scallions and serve.

Did You Know? *Frozen pierogies come in all sorts of flavors, everything from the classic cheddar or onion to traditional old-world favorites like sauerkraut.*

Not Your Grandmother's Sweet Potato Casserole

Grandma's sweet potato casserole is something to be admired, especially when she's generous with the toasted marshmallows. But, sometimes, it's fun to put your own spin on things. That's where this updated version comes in. This one features all that marshmallow-y goodness with an extra-fun, cereal crunch to it. Plus, since we start with refrigerated sweet potatoes, we cut out a lot of the work. No more waiting forever for a taste of this yummy casserole!

Serves 6

Ingredients

1 (28-ounce) package refrigerated mashed sweet potatoes

½ teaspoon salt

1 cup marshmallow crème

1 cup coarsely crushed cornflake cereal

3 tablespoons light brown sugar

2 tablespoon all-purpose flour

2 tablespoons butter, melted

Preparation

1 Preheat oven to 400 degrees F.

2 Place potatoes in a 1-½-quart baking dish; add salt and mix well. Spoon marshmallow crème evenly over potatoes.

3 In a small bowl, combine cereal, brown sugar, flour, and butter; mix well. Sprinkle over marshmallow topping.

4 Bake 20 minutes, or until heated through and the topping is golden.

Test Kitchen Tip: *To help spread the marshmallow cream and prevent it from sticking to the spoon, spray the spoon with non-stick cooking spray.*

Cinnamon-Spiced Skillet Apples

We haven't yet figured out how to add a scratch-n-sniff feature to our books, so you'll have to believe us when we say that these cinnamon-spiced apples smell amazing when they're cooking. Of course, they're pretty darn tasty too. We think this is a great one to serve alongside a pork tenderloin or juicy pork chops. There's just something about the combo of apples and pork that works so well.

Serves 8

Ingredients

½ stick butter

⅓ cup orange juice

6 apples, peeled and sliced into ¼-inch-thick slices

½ cup water

3 teaspoons cornstarch

½ cup brown sugar

½ teaspoon ground cinnamon

¼ teaspoon nutmeg

Orange zest for garnish (optional)

Preparation

1 In a large skillet over medium heat, melt butter. Add orange juice and apples, and cook 8 to 10 minutes, or until apples are fork-tender, stirring occasionally.

2 Meanwhile, whisk water and cornstarch until smooth; slowly stir into apples. Stir in brown sugar, cinnamon, and nutmeg, and heat 2 to 3 minutes, or until sauce is thickened. Garnish with orange zest, if desired. Serve warm.

So Many Options: *Not sure what kind of apples to use in this recipe? Good thing there are plenty of options these days! A few years back we would have recommended Granny Smith apples, since they're firm and tart, but these days, with so many new varieties of apples available, we suggest experimenting with different ones, until you find the ones your family likes best. Just stay away from softer apples, like McIntosh, since they don't hold up well in recipes like this.*

Tropical Island Ambrosia

Most Southerners will tell you this chapter is exactly where this recipe belongs. But in case you're not familiar with their ways or you've never come across ambrosia before, then we're going to fill you in. You see, depending on where you grew up, it's totally normal to have this fruity fluff served alongside savory main dishes. In fact, it's a Southern staple! (Of course, it's up to you whether you bring this out with dinner or save it for dessert. Either way, it's delicious!)

Serves 10

Ingredients

1 (8-ounce) container frozen whipped topping, thawed

1 cup vanilla yogurt

2 cups miniature fruit-flavored marshmallows

1 (11-ounce) can mandarin oranges, drained

1 (8-ounce) can pineapple tidbits, drained

1 cup maraschino cherries, drained

½ cup shredded sweet coconut

½ cup chopped walnuts

Preparation

1 In a large bowl, combine whipped topping and yogurt. Using a rubber spatula, gently fold in remaining ingredients.

2 Serve or refrigerate until ready to serve.

A Little Lighter: *Yes, even a recipe this sinfully good can be lightened up. To do so, start with a lighter whipped topping and fat-free vanilla yogurt. Then, for the canned fruits, you can use the ones with no-sugar-added or those in light syrup.*

On-the-Double Desserts

Molten Chocolate Lava Cakes

Bring on the romance! It's hard not to fall in love with these seductive chocolate cakes that have a creamy chocolate center. After all, chocolate is a well-known aphrodisiac. Make these on date night to share with your special someone and you'll be sure to impress them. (Of course, these are great to share with your family as well, since kids will love how the chocolate spills out when they dig in!)

Makes 4

Ingredients

1 stick butter, plus 1 teaspoon extra for coating ramekins

2 teaspoons all-purpose flour, plus 1 tablespoon extra for dusting ramekins

½ cup semisweet chocolate chips

¼ cup sugar

1 teaspoon vanilla extract

2 eggs

2 egg yolks

Preparation

1 Preheat oven to 425 degrees F. Prepare 4 ramekins or custard cups by coating bottoms and sides with 1 teaspoon of butter and dusting with 1 tablespoon of flour; place on baking sheet.

2 In a microwave-safe bowl, microwave remaining 1 stick butter 1 to 1-½ minutes or until melted. Add chocolate chips and stir until melted and smooth.

3 Add remaining 2 teaspoons flour, the sugar, and vanilla to the chocolate mixture; mix well. Stir in eggs and yolks until smooth. Spoon batter evenly into prepared ramekins.

4 Bake 9 to 10 minutes or until cake is just set and center is soft. Let sit 3 minutes to slightly firm up. (Do not allow to cool or the chocolate center will firm up). Loosen around edges with a knife and remove each to a dessert plate. Serve immediately.

Fancy It Up: We think these are best when served with a dollop of whipped cream and a fresh strawberry to complement the rich chocolaty center.

Lemon-Raspberry Pudding Cake Surprise

Sometimes, the best recipes are born out of one surprising ingredient. In this case, it was one of America's favorite snack cakes. These creamy cakes pair perfectly with the super-bright flavors of lemon and raspberry, creating a dessert that reminds us of summer sunshine, no matter what time of year it's enjoyed.

Serves 9

Ingredients

1 (4-serving size) package instant lemon pudding mix

1-½ cups milk

8 cream-filled sponge snack cakes (see note)

1 (21-ounce) can raspberry pie filling

1 (8-ounce) container frozen whipped topping, thawed

Fresh raspberries and lemon slices for garnish

Preparation

1 In a medium bowl, whisk pudding mix and milk until slightly thickened. Refrigerate 5 minutes.

2 Meanwhile, place cream-filled sponge cakes in an 8-inch square baking dish, arranging them to fit. Spoon chilled pudding evenly over cakes. Layer with pie filling and whipped topping. Garnish with raspberries and lemon slices. Cut into 9 squares and serve. Store leftovers in refrigerator.

Test Kitchen Tip: *We tested these with Twinkies®, but feel free to use any other cream-filled snack cakes you like.*

Blueberry Cheesecake Parfaits

This may be the sweetest way to enjoy those fresh berries you've got sitting in the fridge. Light and fluffy, these pretty parfaits can be whipped up in no time. They're especially great for a hot summer day when you don't feel like turning on the oven. Make them with blueberries, like we did, or use your favorite berries for results that are as delicious as they are darling!

Serves 5

Ingredients

1 (8-ounce) package cream cheese, softened

¾ cup sour cream

1 teaspoon vanilla extract

1 cup confectioners' sugar

1 cup frozen whipped topping, thawed

6 graham cracker sheets, coarsely crushed

2 cups fresh blueberries

Preparation

1 In a medium bowl, combine cream cheese, sour cream, vanilla, and confectioners' sugar; mix until smooth. Fold in whipped topping until thoroughly combined.

2 Divide crushed graham crackers evenly into 5 serving glasses. Spoon half the blueberries and half the cream cheese mixture evenly over graham crackers. Repeat with another layer of blueberries and cream cheese mixture. Serve immediately or refrigerate until ready to serve. Store leftovers in refrigerator.

Weeknight Cheesecake Fondue

After a crazy-busy day at work or school, everyone could use a little pick-me-up. So, why not make an easy family-favorite for dinner and follow it up with a do-it-yourself dessert that's always a whole lot of fun? You can even add on to your fondue spread by setting out bowls of pretzels and fresh fruit to dip along with your cheesecake squares. Not only will you be bringing the family together, but you'll be putting a smile on all of their faces.

Serves 10

Ingredients

1 (8- to 9-inch) frozen cheesecake, slightly thawed

2 cups semisweet chocolate chips

1 teaspoon vegetable oil

Preparation

1 Cut cheesecake into 20 (1-inch) squares and place on a platter.

2 In a medium microwave-safe bowl, combine chocolate chips and oil. Microwave 1-½ minutes, or until chips are melted and mixture is smooth, stirring occasionally. Place melted chocolate in a fondue pot with a candle or sterno light under it to keep warm.

3 Skewer pieces of the cheesecake with fondue forks or bamboo skewers and dip into warm, chocolate fondue.

7-Layer Raspberry Torte

A torte is simply a type of cake that's denser and has more layers than the average cake. Some people argue that a torte is usually fancier than most cakes, but we're not taking sides. All we know is that our 7-layer torte is a real crowd-pleaser. It has a tendency to make people "ooh" and "aah" from the moment it's put on the table.

Serves 10

Ingredients

1 (16-ounce) frozen pound cake, thawed

½ cup raspberry preserves

¾ cup chocolate chips

½ cup heavy cream

¼ cup sliced almonds

Preparation

1 With a serrated knife, cut the pound cake horizontally into 4 even layers. Place the bottom layer on a wire cooling rack over a baking sheet and spread ⅓ of the preserves evenly over the layer, then top with next piece of pound cake. Repeat 2 more times, then top with the final layer of pound cake.

2 Place the chocolate chips in a medium bowl. Heat heavy cream in a small saucepan over medium-low heat until hot, but not boiling. Pour the hot cream over chips and stir until melted and smooth, creating a chocolate ganache.

3 Pour the ganache evenly over top and sides of the cake, then sprinkle almonds on top. Place on a serving platter and refrigerate 10 minutes or until ready to serve. Store leftovers in refrigerator.

Fancy It Up: *Garnish with a few fresh raspberries to make this look extra-fancy!*

Chocolate Funnel Cakes

Go ahead and do your happy dance because...oh yeah, funnel cakes! And not just regular funnel cakes, but chocolaty, crispy, sprinkled-with-lots-of-powdered-sugar funnel cakes that you can totally make at home! No more waiting for the fair to come to town and no more long lines at the carnival. The fried dough you love so much is yours for the taking!

Serves 5

Ingredients

1-⅓ cups all-purpose flour

½ cup granulated sugar

¼ cup cocoa powder

1 teaspoon baking soda

1 teaspoon baking powder

½ teaspoon salt

1 egg

1 cup milk

½ teaspoon vanilla extract

Oil for frying

Confectioners' sugar for sprinkling

Preparation

1 In a large bowl, whisk flour, sugar, cocoa powder, baking soda, baking powder, and salt; mix well. In a medium bowl, whisk egg, milk, and vanilla until well blended. Add to flour mixture and whisk until smooth.

2 In a medium saucepan over medium-high heat, heat 1-inch of oil until hot, but not smoking.

3 Holding a finger over the bottom of a funnel with a ⅝-inch opening, pour ½ cup of batter into funnel. Remove finger and drizzle batter into hot oil, swirling it in circles from the center outward. (You'll only make one at a time and each should be the size of the saucepan.) Fry 1 to 2 minutes on each side or until set.

4 Drain on paper towels and sprinkle with confectioners' sugar. Repeat until all batter is used. Serve warm.

Test Kitchen Tip: *Make sure you use the batter right after making it or it will thicken up and won't flow freely through the funnel. If it does get too thick, mix a little milk into the batter until it flows freely again.*

Buttery Biscuit Apple Cobbler

You know what they say, "An apple a day keeps the doctor away." If you've run out of ways to get your apples in, then here's a sweet idea. This apple cobbler is warm and comforting, especially since it's topped with a layer of buttery biscuits. We like to serve this old-fashioned favorite the way moms have been serving it for years, with a scoop of ice cream or a dollop of freshly whipped cream. It's just so good!

Serves 6

Ingredients

6 tablespoons butter, divided

½ cup light brown sugar

2 teaspoons cornstarch

1 teaspoon ground cinnamon, divided

5 Granny Smith apples, peeled, cored, and thinly sliced

1 (10.2-ounce) can refrigerated biscuits, each cut into 6 pieces

Preparation

1 Preheat oven to 425 degrees F.

2 In a large cast iron or oven-safe skillet over medium-high heat, melt 4 tablespoons butter, then add brown sugar, cornstarch, ½ teaspoon cinnamon, and the apples. Cook 5 minutes, stirring occasionally.

3 Meanwhile, in a medium bowl melt remaining 2 tablespoons butter. Add biscuit pieces and remaining ½ teaspoon cinnamon; toss until evenly coated. Place biscuits on top of apples.

4 Bake 10 to 15 minutes, or until biscuits are golden. Serve piping hot. Store leftovers in refrigerator.

Test Kitchen Tip: *An easy way to cut the raw biscuit dough is with a pair of kitchen shears.*

Juicy Peaches Skillet Crumble

You'll love this quick alternative to peach pie. Our peach crumble features a thick and buttery oat and graham cracker crumb topping that's unlike any other you've had before. And since this recipe can be made with frozen or fresh peaches, you can make it when the mood strikes you (even when you're wishing for summer in the winter!). As you'll soon find out, sometimes the best desserts are the simplest ones.

Serves 5

Ingredients

5 tablespoons butter, divided

¾ cup light brown sugar, divided

1 [16-ounce] package frozen peaches, thawed

3 graham cracker sheets, coarsely crushed

⅓ cup quick-cooking oats

½ teaspoon ground cinnamon

Preparation

1 In a large skillet over medium heat, melt 2 tablespoons butter and ½ cup brown sugar. Add peaches and cook 4 to 5 minutes or until heated through.

2 Meanwhile, in a small skillet over medium heat, melt remaining 3 tablespoons butter. Add crushed graham crackers, oats, cinnamon, and the remaining ¼ cup brown sugar. Heat 2 to 3 minutes, stirring occasionally until the mixture starts to caramelize.

3 Sprinkle oat mixture over peaches and serve. Store leftovers in refrigerator.

Test Kitchen Tip: *If you want to use fresh peaches when they're in season, simply peel them, cut into slices, and sauté until tender. You'll need about 4 to 5 cups of sliced peaches.*

Maple-icious Pecan Pie Trifle

This show-stopping dessert requires absolutely no special skills whatsoever, yet it always earns loads of compliments. You can throw this one together last minute using your favorite store-bought pecan pie. When layered with the delicious combo of whipped topping and maple syrup (plus chocolate chips!), you've got yourself the makings of a remarkable dessert for any occasion. Be sure to bring plenty of spoons to the table, because everyone is going to want some.

Serves 10

Ingredients

1 (9-inch) store-bought pecan pie, thawed if frozen

1 (8-ounce) container whipped topping

2 tablespoons maple syrup

2 tablespoons mini chocolate chips

Preparation

1 Cut the pie into 1-inch pieces.

2 In a medium bowl, combine whipped topping and maple syrup; set aside.

3 Place ⅓ of the pie pieces into a medium serving bowl. Spoon half the whipped topping mixture over the pie pieces, then sprinkle with 1 tablespoon chocolate chips. Repeat with another layer of pie pieces and whipped topping mixture, then finish with a layer of pie pieces and the remaining 1 tablespoon chocolate chips.

4 Serve immediately or refrigerate until ready to serve. Store leftovers in refrigerator.

Test Kitchen Tip: *If you want to substitute the whipped topping with homemade whipped cream, make sure you add the maple syrup after it is whipped well. Otherwise, the cream might not whip to the desired stiffness. As for the pie, it can be a frozen one or one you get in the bakery section.*

Deconstructed
Apple Pie à la Mode

When you think about the best apple pie you've ever eaten, what do you think about first? Is it the flaky crust or is it the gooey apple filling that spills out when you dig your fork in? For everyone in the Test Kitchen, it was something different. Inspired by all the individual "parts" that make an apple pie so memorable, we came up with this deconstructed version that's faster to make and features everything you love…including the ice cream!

Serves 5

Ingredients

3 tablespoons sugar

1 teaspoon ground cinnamon

1 refrigerated rolled pie crust (from a 14.1-ounce package)

2 tablespoons butter, melted

1 (21-ounce) can apple pie filling

1 quart vanilla ice cream

Preparation

1 Preheat oven to 400 degrees F. Line a baking sheet with wax paper.

2 In a small bowl, combine sugar and cinnamon; mix well. Unroll the pie crust on a cutting board and brush half the butter evenly on top. Sprinkle evenly with half the sugar mixture. Flip the crust over and repeat the steps, so both sides are evenly coated. Cut into 1- x 3-inch strips and place on baking sheet.

3 Bake 8 to 10 minutes or until golden and crisp.

4 Meanwhile, pour pie filling into a microwave-safe bowl and microwave about 2 minutes, or until warm. Evenly divide pie filling into serving dishes, top each with a scoop of ice cream, and place 2 pie crust sticks into bowl. Serve immediately. Store extra pie crust sticks in an airtight container.

Test Kitchen Tip: *Since one pie crust makes about 30 pie crust sticks, you'll have some left over. You can store them in an airtight container, so that they're ready for you the next time you have a craving, or you can serve yourself more than the suggested two, if that's your preference. These are so crispy and delicious, it's hard to resist them!*

Coconut Cream Mini Pies

Serve these indulgent treats after dinner and watch your family go "coconuts" over them! These mini pies will send their taste buds straight to heaven with just a couple of bites. Who says a little dessert can't satisfy a big sweet tooth? Just wait till the compliments come pouring in. You'll be making these all the time!

Makes 6

Ingredients

1 refrigerated rolled pie crust (from a 14.1-ounce package)

¼ cup shredded coconut

1 (4-serving size) package instant coconut cream pudding mix

1-½ cups milk

1-½ cups whipped topping

Preparation

1 Preheat oven to 450 degrees F.

2 Unroll pie crust on a cutting board. Cut 6 (3-½-inch) circles out of crust. (See note.) Place the circles in the bottom and up the sides of 6 muffin tin cups.

3 Bake 8 to 9 minutes or until golden. Carefully remove pie crusts from muffin tin cups and let cool.

4 Spread coconut on a baking sheet and bake 3 to 4 minutes or until golden. (Keep an eye on it, because it browns quickly.)

5 Meanwhile, in a medium bowl, whisk pudding mix and milk until slightly thickened. Refrigerate 5 minutes. Fill cooled pie crusts with pudding and top evenly with whipped topping. Sprinkle with toasted coconut. Enjoy right away or refrigerate until ready to serve. Store leftovers in refrigerator.

Test Kitchen Tip: *If you don't have a 3-1/2-inch round cookie cutter, just grab a ruler and find a drinking glass, coffee mug, plastic storage container, or clean can that's about the right size. Then, place that on the dough and use it as a template to cut out each circle with a paring knife.*

Oh My Goodness! Chocolate Seduction

Death by Chocolate was one of Art Ginsburg's ("Mr. Food," our founder) favorite desserts. And today, it's still one of our most popular recipes online. It's a dessert that always makes people cry out, "Oh my goodness!" since it's loaded with so much decadent chocolate. We decided to update this classic by making it smaller, so you can enjoy it with a more intimate crowd of people. Just be careful, this one has a reputation for being seductive.

Serves 8

Ingredients

1 (4-serving size) package instant chocolate pudding mix

1-½ cups milk

8 store-bought brownies, broken up into 1-inch pieces

1 (8-ounce) container frozen whipped topping, thawed

2 (1.4-ounce) bars chocolate-covered toffee candy, coarsely crushed

Preparation

1 In a medium bowl, whisk pudding mix and milk until slightly thickened. Refrigerate 5 minutes.

2 Place brownie pieces in a 9-inch deep dish pie plate. Spoon pudding evenly over brownies. Top with a layer of whipped topping, then sprinkle with candy. Serve or chill until ready to serve. Store leftovers in refrigerator.

Finishing Touch: *To take this totally over the top, drizzle the brownies with chocolate or coffee liqueur before assembling. Just be warned, if you decide to go this route, we can't be held responsible for how wild and crazy anyone who indulges in this will behave.*

Almond-Kissed Coconut Macaroons

You can make more with sliced bread than a sandwich; you can also make these cookies! That's right, with some basic pantry staples, you've got the ingredients to make your new favorite go-to cookie recipe. No one will believe what you've made them with, but, trust us, they won't be complaining as they gobble up one after the other. (Psst. These make a great gift too!)

Makes 24

Ingredients

1 (14-ounce) can sweetened condensed milk

1 (7-ounce) package sweetened flaked coconut (about 1-2/3 cups)

2 cups fresh bread crumbs (about 4 slices bread) (see note)

1 teaspoon almond extract

24 whole almonds

Preparation

1 Preheat oven to 350 degrees F. Coat rimmed baking sheets with cooking spray.

2 In a large bowl, combine all ingredients except almonds; mix well.

3 Drop mixture by rounded tablespoonfuls onto baking sheets. Press an almond into center of each macaroon.

4 Bake 13 to 15 minutes or until edges are golden. Cool at least 5 minutes before serving. Store in an airtight container.

Test Kitchen Tip: *To make the fresh bread crumbs, you can either grate the slices of fresh bread or place them in a food processor with a cutting blade and process until they are finely chopped.*

Chocolate Chip Freckle Cookies

No, these cookies didn't earn their freckles from sitting out too long in the oven. The freckles we're talking about in this recipe are actually chocolate chips, and there's two kinds here! So, what do you get when you've got double the chocolate goodness? Well, aside from a party in your mouth, you've also got the most dangerously addictive cookies in the world. (We don't think we're exaggerating at all.)

Makes 2 dozen

Ingredients

1-½ cups all-purpose flour

1 teaspoon baking soda

½ teaspoon salt

1 stick butter, softened

⅓ cup granulated sugar

⅓ cup packed light brown sugar

1 teaspoon vanilla extract

1 egg

½ cup semisweet chocolate chips

½ cup white chocolate chips

½ cup chopped walnuts

Preparation

1 Preheat oven to 375 degrees F.

2 In a medium bowl, combine flour, baking soda, and salt; set aside.

3 In a large bowl, combine butter, granulated sugar, brown sugar, and vanilla; beat until creamy. Beat in egg, then gradually add flour mixture until well combined. Stir in the chips and nuts; mix well.

4 Drop mixture by rounded teaspoonfuls onto ungreased baking sheets.

5 Bake 8 to 10 minutes or until golden. Cool 2 minutes, then remove cookies to a wire rack to cool completely. Store in an airtight container until ready to serve.

Test Kitchen Tip: *Make sure that you don't grease the baking sheets. If you do, the batter will spread more while baking and you'll end up with flat cookies.*

Red Velvet Crinkles with White Chocolate Chips

We'd like to nominate these cookies for "Most Likely to Disappear from the Cookie Jar First," because, well, these crinkly, chocolaty, and velvety cookies never seem to stick around for long. As soon as they see them, everyone will be reaching for them! Good thing for you, these cookies start with a box of cake mix, so you can easily bake up another batch whenever the jar is running low.

Makes 24

Ingredients

½ cup confectioners' sugar

1 teaspoon cornstarch

1 package red velvet cake mix

6 tablespoons butter, melted

1 egg, beaten

½ cup white chocolate chips

Preparation

1 Preheat oven to 375 degrees F.

2 In a shallow dish, mix confectioners' sugar and cornstarch; set aside.

3 In a large bowl, combine cake mix, butter, and egg; mix well. Stir in chips. Roll into 1-inch balls, then roll balls in sugar mixture. Place on a baking sheet.

4 Bake 10 to 11 minutes or until set. Let cool 1 to 2 minutes on baking sheet before removing to a wire rack to cool completely. Store in an airtight container.

Test Kitchen Tip: *We tested this with several brands of cake mix, from national brands to store brands, and the results were consistently delicious. So, go ahead and use whatever brand you like best.*

Gotta-Have S'mores Squares

Honestly, who has time to build a fire every time they get the urge to eat s'mores? Not us! And let's face it, that isn't stopping us from making one of our favorite ooey-gooey treats of all time. Instead, we've improvised by creating this easy-peasy version that's perfect for those "gotta-have" moments. (P.S. There's no roasting sticks needed.)

Makes 20

Ingredients

½ stick butter

1 (10-ounce) package mini marshmallows, with ¼ cup reserved for topping

7 cups graham cracker cereal (see note)

4 (1.55-ounce) chocolate candy bars, separated into sections

Preparation

1 Preheat broiler. Coat a 9- x 13-inch baking dish with cooking spray.

2 In a large saucepan over low heat, melt butter. Add marshmallows (don't forget to set aside ¼ cup for later) and stir until completely melted. Remove from heat. Add cereal and mix until evenly coated.

3 Using a spatula, press half the cereal mixture into the baking dish. Top with half the chocolate candy. Spoon remaining cereal mixture on top, pressing down lightly. Top with remaining chocolate candy. Sprinkle the reserved ¼ cup of marshmallows evenly over top.

4 Place baking dish on middle oven rack and broil 1 to 2 minutes, or until marshmallows are golden. Place in refrigerator 15 minutes to firm up, then cut into 20 squares. Store leftovers in an airtight container.

Test Kitchen Tip: *To make it easier to spread the sticky cereal mixture, spray the spatula with cooking spray. It should make spreading and clean up a breeze. We tested this recipe using Golden Grahams® cereal.*

Pumpkin Pie Roll-Ups

Now you can have pumpkin pie anytime, not just in the fall or during the holidays! These easy roll-ups come together super-quick and have all that pumpkin spice flavor that's so popular these days. We've even added a simple glaze for a little extra "yum!" They're great for a busy weeknight or can be served with breakfast as a sweet pastry with a glass of milk or a cup of coffee.

Makes 8

Ingredients

½ cup canned pure pumpkin

1 egg yolk

1-½ tablespoons granulated sugar

½ teaspoon pumpkin pie spice

1 (8-ounce) package refrigerated crescent rolls

½ cup confectioners' sugar

1 tablespoon milk

Preparation

1 Preheat oven to 375 degrees F.

2 In a small bowl, combine pumpkin, egg yolk, granulated sugar, and pumpkin pie spice; mix well.

3 Unroll dough, separate into triangles, and place 1 teaspoon pumpkin mixture on the wide end of each piece of the crescent dough. Starting with wide end, roll the dough over the filling, bring up the sides (so the filling won't ooze out), and then continue to roll up. Place on baking sheet seam-side down.

4 Bake 10 to 12 minutes or until golden. Remove to a wire rack.

5 Meanwhile, in a small bowl, whisk confectioners' sugar and milk until smooth. Drizzle glaze over crescent rolls and serve warm. Store in an airtight container.

PB & Chocolate Dessert Bars

Did you know that peanut butter cups are one of America's favorite candies? Year after year this flavor combo sneaks its way into our Valentine's Day boxes, our Easter baskets, and our Halloween goodie bags...and no one is complaining. In fact, if anything, everyone wants more! Well, here's how you can have more without having to run to the store every time. These dessert bars are 5-ingredient simple and ready to satisfy.

Makes 30

Ingredients

1 cup creamy peanut butter

2 sticks butter, melted

1 pound confectioners' sugar

1-½ cups graham cracker crumbs

2 cups semisweet chocolate chips

Preparation

1 Coat a 10- x 15-inch rimmed baking sheet with cooking spray.

2 In a large bowl, combine peanut butter, butter, confectioners' sugar, and graham cracker crumbs; mix with a wooden spoon until mixture becomes stiff. Spread on baking sheet.

3 In a medium microwave-safe bowl, melt chocolate chips 90 seconds or until smooth. Spread chocolate evenly over peanut butter mixture.

4 Place in the freezer for 15 minutes to firm up. Cut into 30 bars. Store leftovers in refrigerator.

Did You Know? *These dessert bars will last about 6 months in the freezer (that is, if you can go that long without eating them all first!). Just make sure you wrap them well in wax paper, and place them in a freezer storage bag, so they don't get freezer burn.*

Short & Sweet Praline Squares

We'll keep this short and sweet. These praline squares are the perfect treat for when you're craving something sweet. Their delicious pecan crunch makes them great for sharing with friends or for keeping all to yourself (just make sure you hide them well, because once they get a taste....well, there's no stopping them after that).

Makes 24

Ingredients

24 graham cracker sheets

2 sticks butter

1 cup packed light brown sugar

1 cup chopped pecans

Preparation

1 Preheat oven to 350 degrees F. On a 10- x 15-inch rimmed baking sheet, place graham crackers, so that they touch each other.

2 In a small saucepan over medium heat, bring butter and brown sugar to a boil; cook 4 minutes or until mixture begins to caramelize, stirring constantly. (Be careful, this mixture will be very hot!) Stir in nuts; mix well. Spoon mixture evenly over graham crackers.

3 Bake 8 minutes. Remove from oven and let cool on baking sheet 5 minutes. Refrigerate 5 minutes, then cut into 24 squares. Store in an airtight container.

Fun Fact: How do you pronounce the word "pecan"? The most popular way to say it is, "pee-KAHN," but in many areas of the South it's more common to say, "pick-AHN," and if you ask someone along the east coast, you might hear them say, "PEE-can." No matter how you say it, pecans are perfect in these praline squares!

Sweet & Salty Anytime Bars

Here's a list of times when it's appropriate to eat these dessert bars: at birthday parties or when you're feeling blue, at baby showers or when the day is finally through, at picnics or when you're feeling glad, at potlucks or when you're feeling mad... Do you get the idea? The point is, these are good anytime, anyplace. So, make them when you want and enjoy every sweet and salty bite.

Makes 18

Ingredients

3 cups semisweet chocolate chips

1-½ cups coarsely crushed pretzels

1 cup crispy rice cereal

1 (10-½-ounce) package miniature marshmallows

Preparation

1 Lightly coat a 9- x 13-inch baking dish with cooking spray.

2 In a large microwave-safe bowl, melt chocolate chips 2 minutes, or until melted and smooth, stirring as needed. Add pretzels and cereal; mix well. Stir in marshmallows until well coated. Spread mixture evenly in baking dish.

3 Refrigerate 20 minutes, then cut into 18 bars. Store leftovers in refrigerator.

Test Kitchen Tip: *If you have a super big bag of mini marshmallows, you'll only need 6-½ cups for this recipe. (Psst. If you want to add some extra marshmallows on top, go ahead!)*

Gourmet-Style Mocha Truffles

Here's something you may not have known before: coffee is often used in chocolate desserts, since it makes the flavor more intense. In the case of these gourmet-style truffles, we added just enough coffee to bring out the richness of the chocolate while still being able to experience some of the mocha flavor. These truffles are great as an everyday treat, but are also fancy enough to be displayed on special occasions and gifted during the holidays.

Makes 18

Ingredients

2 tablespoons water

1 tablespoon instant coffee granules

¾ cup semisweet chocolate chips

¾ cup ground almonds

¾ cup confectioners' sugar, divided

Preparation

1 In a medium saucepan over medium heat, combine water and coffee granules, stirring until granules are dissolved. Add chocolate chips and stir until melted.

2 Remove from heat and stir in almonds and ½ cup confectioners' sugar until thoroughly combined. Shape into 18 (1-inch) balls, then roll in remaining ¼ cup confectioners' sugar.

3 Place on baking sheet and chill 10 minutes or until firm. Serve or store in an airtight container until ready to serve.

Test Kitchen Tip: *To make each truffle perfectly round and about the same size, we recommend using a small ice cream scoop. You can pick one up for a few dollars wherever kitchen tools are sold. Not only is it good for truffles, but it's also handy for everything from making cocktail-sized meatballs to balling fresh melons for a colorful fruit salad.*

Candy Bar Cookie Dough

Finally—a cookie dough you can eat without baking! After listening to one of our Test Kitchen team members describe how his mom used to slap his hands away from the bowl for trying to sneak a fingerful of raw dough, we decided to do him a favor and came up with a tummy-friendly version that even Mom would approve of (no eggs!). This cookie dough is the stuff of dreams, especially since we made it doubly-good by adding candy bar pieces!

Serves 8

Ingredients

1 stick butter, softened

¾ cup light brown sugar

1 teaspoon vanilla extract

1 cup all-purpose flour

¼ teaspoon salt

2 tablespoons milk

¼ cup semisweet chocolate chips

1 cup coarsely chopped chocolate candy bars (see note)

Preparation

1 In a large bowl with an electric mixer, beat butter, brown sugar, and vanilla until creamy. Add flour and salt, and mix until crumbly. Add milk; mix well. Stir in chocolate chips and candy.

2 Enjoy right away or refrigerate until ready to serve.

So Many Options: *As for the type of candy bars to use, feel free to mix and match. We used Butterfingers® and Snickers® candy bars when we tested this. You could even toss in some chopped nuts, if you prefer.*

Nutty Bananas Foster Ice Cream Balls

Bananas Foster is one of life's most clap-worthy desserts. We say "clap-worthy" because whenever it's ordered at a restaurant, and served tableside, it always puts on a show and people always clap. There's just something about watching the waiter set a fire at your table that's pretty mesmerizing. This recipe doesn't include the pyrotechnics, but it does have all the same legendary results. We even added a little crunch to our version to give it extra texture and taste.

Makes 6

Ingredients

2 cups toasted cornflakes with nut clusters cereal, crushed (see note)

½ teaspoon ground cinnamon

1 quart vanilla ice cream

½ stick butter

½ cup light brown sugar

2 tablespoons rum (optional)

3 bananas, sliced

Preparation

1 In a shallow dish, combine cereal and cinnamon; mix well and set aside.

2 With an ice cream scoop, form 6 ice cream balls, each about 2-½ inches in diameter. Roll ice cream in cereal mixture, coating on all sides. Place ice cream balls in a 9- x 13-inch baking dish, then place in freezer.

3 In a medium skillet over medium heat, melt butter; add brown sugar and cook until sugar is dissolved, stirring constantly. Add rum, if desired, and bananas, and cook 2 to 3 minutes or until bananas are softened.

4 When ready to serve, place ice cream balls in shallow bowls and top with banana mixture. Serve immediately.

Test Kitchen Tip: *The best way to crush the cereal without making a mess is to place it in a resealable plastic bag. After removing the air from the bag, crush the cereal by rolling over it with a rolling pin or the side of a soup can. Oh, and by the way, we tested this recipe with Honey Bunches of Oats® cereal, but you can substitute with a different brand, if you prefer.*

Hazelnut Mousse Chocolate-Dipped Cones

We swapped out the ice cream in these nutty, chocolate-dipped cones in favor of a creamy, decadent, hazelnut mousse that'll put you over the moon. Cute as can be and simple to make, these ice cream cone look-a-likes are a treat for days when you could use a little extra cheer. (Isn't that every day?) And, instead of a cherry on top, we went with a raspberry, since it goes so well with the flavors of the mousse and provides a nice pop of color!

Makes 4

Ingredients

½ cup chocolate-hazelnut spread (see note)

1 (8-ounce) container frozen whipped topping, thawed

¼ cup chopped walnuts

½ cup semi-sweet chocolate chips

4 sugar ice cream cones

Fresh raspberries for garnish

Preparation

1 In a medium bowl, prepare the mousse filling by folding chocolate-hazelnut spread into whipped topping until thoroughly combined; refrigerate until chilled.

2 Meanwhile, place walnuts in a shallow bowl or saucer. In a medium microwave-safe bowl, microwave chocolate chips 45 to 60 seconds or until melted and smooth. Dip top ½-inch of cone into chocolate, then roll in nuts. Place cones in a glass to hold upright.

3 Place mousse into a large resealable plastic bag or a pastry bag with a star tip. If using a resealable bag, cut off one corner of the bag and pipe the mousse into each cone. Top with a raspberry and serve immediately, or refrigerate until ready to serve.

Test Kitchen Tip: *We tested this recipe using Nutella®, but you can use any other chocolate-hazelnut spread you prefer.*

Banana Split Ice Cream Crepes

Don't think for a split second that you're going to be able to resist this dessert! Everything about these says, "Eat me!" and really, since they're so easy, there's nothing that should be stopping you. You could almost think of this as an "upgrade" from your typical banana split. But the real cherry on top here is that there's no baking or extra work to be done. Just assemble and grab a spoon!

Serves 4

Ingredients

1 (1.5-quart) container vanilla ice cream (see note)

4 (9-inch) ready-to-use crepes (from a 5-ounce package)

1 banana, sliced

1 cup hot fudge, warmed

2 cups whipped cream

4 maraschino cherries, drained well

¼ cup chopped walnuts (optional)

Preparation

1 Using scissors, cut open one end of the ice cream container, and slide ice cream onto a cutting board. Cut 2 "slices," lengthwise, each about 1-inch thick. Then, cut each slice in half, creating 4 ice cream logs. Place remaining ice cream back in the packaging, wrap well, and freeze for another use.

2 Place ice cream log in center of each crepe and roll up, placing seam-side down on dessert plates.

3 Top each crepe evenly with banana slices, hot fudge, whipped cream, cherries, and walnuts, if desired. Serve immediately.

Test Kitchen Tip: *The easiest way to make these is to start with ice cream that comes in the old-fashioned square blocks. If that's not convenient for you, you can always place three small scoops of ice cream in each crepe and then roll them up.*

Make-Your-Own Ice Cream Sandwiches

I scream, you scream, we all scream for...ice cream! Here's a fun recipe that the whole family can get involved with. Set out the toppings buffet-style and let everyone make their own creations. You can even play some familiar ice cream truck tunes in the background to make the mood even merrier. This is a great way to bring everyone together!

Makes 8

Ingredients

1 (16.5-ounce) package refrigerated chocolate chip cookie dough

1 quart peanut butter cup ice cream

Assorted toppings such as sprinkles, chopped nuts, or mini chocolate chips (optional)

Preparation

1 Preheat oven to 350 degrees F. Using a sharp knife, cut cookie dough into 16 slices and place on a baking sheet.

2 Bake 9 minutes, or until brown around edges. After cooling a minute or so, remove cookies to a wire rack to cool completely, about 10 minutes.

3 Meanwhile, allow ice cream to soften slightly, then place 1 small scoop on the flat side of a cookie; place another cookie flat-side down over ice cream. Squeeze the 2 cookies together until ice cream is pushed to the edges. Repeat until 8 sandwiches are formed.

4 If desired, place toppings on a plate and roll edges of sandwiches over them, pressing lightly so toppings stick. Serve immediately or wrap individually in plastic wrap, and keep frozen until ready to serve.

So Many Options: We know there's no reason to tell you this, but just as a reminder, feel free to swap out the flavor of the ice cream for whatever your family prefers best. You might even want to make a whole variety of them, so everyone will have their favorite flavor on hand when they get a craving.

Brownie Waffle Turtle Sundaes

Instead of taking your family out for ice cream, how about serving them an ice cream shop favorite right at home? Better yet, surprise them with a sundae unlike any other! The base for these is a brownie that's made in a waffle iron, which means that everyone gets a crispy "edge" piece. Not only does it look fun, but it tastes awesome. A scoop of ice cream, a generous drizzle of caramel, and a sprinkle of pecans, and you've just put together something magical.

Serves 8

Ingredients

1 package brownie mix

1 quart vanilla caramel swirl ice cream

1 cup caramel sauce

½ cup chopped pecans

Preparation

1 Prepare brownie batter according to package directions.

2 Meanwhile, preheat an electric waffle iron according to manufacturer's directions. Coat with cooking spray. Pour about ¾ cup batter onto bottom of waffle iron. Close lid and cook 2 to 2-½ minutes, or until set. Carefully remove waffle to a plate. Repeat with remaining batter.

3 Top each waffle with a scoop of ice cream. Drizzle with caramel sauce and sprinkle with pecans. Serve immediately.

Test Kitchen Tip: *Depending on the size of your waffle maker, you may make one or two extra waffles. You can freeze these for another time you're craving something decadent like this. And if your waffles are really big, you may even choose to use only a half of a waffle for each serving.*

Index